# Drone On!
## The High History of Celtic Music

Winnie Czulinski

Sound And Vision

# Table of Contents

# A Glib Glossary

Bard: Poet, harper or singer, sometimes barred

Beag: Small, as in "*ceol beag*," "everyday music"

Beltane: Ancient spring festival of May 1

Bodhran: Hand-held Irish framed drum

Bombarde: Love-it-or-hate-it Breton wind instrument

Bouzouki: Greek-cum-Celtic stringed instrument

Caoineadh: Vocal or instrumental lament

Canntaireachd: Bagpipe-teaching vocal sounds

Ceili(dh): Boisterous gathering, often with music

Craic: A certain "spirit" found in bars & gatherings

Danu: Ancient Celtic mother-goddess, re: Danube River

Drone: Underlying single tone in some instruments

Druid: Ancient Celtic version of a very learned wizard

Feis(anna): Sneezy & stiff-spined Irish dance event(s).

Fleadh: Festival with more sneezing, lots of music

Gaita: Bagpipes or badpipes in Galicia (nw. Spain)

Gentraige: Music to get happy and party to

Goltraige: Music to get depressed with

Hurdy-gurdy: Wind-it-up keys-&-drone instrument

Jig: Fast dance or tune in a 6/8, 9/8, 12/8 rhythm

Keltoi: Ancient Greek term for the Celts

Lugh: Ancient Celtic hot-head who ruled the sun

Mhor: Big as in "Oran Mhor," a song of the Universe

Mode: A sequence of a seven-note musical scale

Muckle Sang: Old Scottish ballad not to be mucked up

Needfire: Ancient communal fire everyone lit up from

Pandeireteras: Galician gals who run with tambourines

Piobaireachd: Highfalutin music for Highland bagpipes

Planxty: A song composed specially for a patron

Puirt a beul: Gaelic for garbled "mouth music"

Reel: A dance or tune, usually in 4/4 rhythm

Sid(d)he: Fairy(ies), pronounced "she," but often a "he"

Suantraige: Sleep-perchance-to-dream music

Tuatha de Danaan: Ancient tribe of warrior-gods

Uillean ("elbow") pipes: Bellows-blown badpipes

*

5

# Author's Introduction

This subject began to crack me up some time ago. Crack is the right word, too, as it's the pronunciation of the Gaelic word *craic*. And *craic* is nothing less than a certain spontaneous spirit that happens when you stir up good music, grand emotions and great PR.

It's the kind of thing you can blame for 2005 & 2006 marking the 10th anniversaries of *Riverdance* and *Lord of the Dance*. Not only did these shows erupt with Gael force, they've had to clone themselves to meet global demand, and have inspired a torrent of competing Celt-athons.

*Riverdance, Lord of the Dance* and a Canadian Celtic show called *Needfire* exploded into my existence about the time I first picked up an instrument called the mountain dulcimer. From the start, these dual experiences twisted themselves around each other in a kind of warped weave I now know I'm entangled within for eternity.

As I became a musician, I learned what's really behind *Riverdance* is about 3,000-years-old, is as mythical as historical, and infects much of the globe. And my dulcimer – an all-in-one music-maker that thinks it's a stringed bagpipe, can be played with a violin bow and is an affair of the harp – was my multiCeltural gateway into it all.

As I began musically documenting my own journey and that of the Celts, I also began to be aware of the potential humor in Celtic music history. Be warned: This book weaves in and out among past, present, future and past imperfect. In pleading my case, I can only compare my approach to Celtic design, which goes all over the place but does have a pattern.

But first – I make my stand for "Keltic," not "Seltic." Herodotus and other ancient learned Greeks named these rampaging ranters the *Keltoi*, meaning the "not one of us" of a loose linguistic group. And having once seen and heard *Riverdance*, there's no way anyone could conceive of Celtic with a soft C. Yes, the Celts have left us some soft lyrical stuff. But overall, they've made just too much of an impact not to be hard as well as heard.

**

## Dedication

To my father Tadeusz (1913-2001),
who loved *Riverdance*.
My mother Winifred.
And to Ken Bilton and Dave King,
true friends in music.

\*\*\*

# Chapter 1

# Horning and Hollering into Hystery

Some time before 1000 BCE, the Celts rose up out of the headwaters of the Eastern European *Danuvius* or Danube River, named after the mother-goddess Danu. They shook themselves off before the sun, invented some weapons, tried out their voices, stamped their feet, drank a toast for posterity and were off.

This motley collection of Indo-European tribes with horned helmets and horrendous warhorns began to thunder and reel over most of the known world, stopping off for a role in Biblical times. In Paul's letter to the Galatians, Celts who had settled in Gaul, he urged them to "avoid idolatry, sorcery, hatred and murder." In other words, all the stuff that made for really good songs. Fortunately, the Celts seem to have ignored Paul's pleas, and musicians and music-lovers, parading pipe bands and dancers everywhere are reaping the benefits of that rebellion.

The ancient Celts were whooping it up in places like France, Germany, Switzerland, Scandinavia, Greece, possibly Africa and even China, but they left the longest-running musical evidence in Ireland, Scotland, Wales, Cornwall, The Isle of Man, Brittany and Celtic Spain, as well as ultimately in North America, from Newfoundland to Nashville.

Still, it's obvious the Celts were "doing it" with whomever they came across in their multicultural hystery tour.

How else to explain the similarity of the mystical terms *siddhartha* (Hindu/Buddhist) and *siddhe* (hinterland-Irish)? Or the fact that the bad guy in *Lord of the Dance* is called Don Dorcha (dark lord), same way Brando was bowed to as Don Corleone in *The Godfather*?

First-century BCE scholar Diodorus thought the Celts were great dramatists if noisy and other people think they're just noisy, but they've given us a legacy of music that's universal, timeless, endlessly re-invented – and does have some Ps and Qs. In Celtic linguistics, P stands for the Celtic "Brythonic" languages of Welsh, Cornish and Breton, and Q for Celtic "Goidelic" of Scottish, Irish and Manx, while Celtic-Spanish stands alone. There's a lot to be said about any of these lands, but a potty history follows, starting with:

## IRELAND

Also known as Eire, Eireann, Erin and Aisling, it first was settled by Celts called Milesians from Spain and Egypt and is famous for stepdancing, fairies called *sidhe* (shee), harps on beer bottles and warrior heroes known for their great lays, or ballads.

Music was a relative thing, with families like the O'Dalys, who were higher than anyone else in the 12th century, because they went back to Conn of the Hundred Battles in the second century. The O'Dalys were the type to split someone's head with an axe, then immediately sing a poem about it, and nothing could better illustrate the Celts' dual war-and-literature leanings.

This also was due to the parti-influences of Vikings and French knights who came muscling in to create some Pan-Celtic. By the 14th century or so, this musical melting pot began to suffer, when the Crown started passing statutes to clamp down on any music remotely Celtic, a recurring theme throughout this history.

It didn't quite work, and by the 18th century Irish music was a knotty tapestry of fiddling, piping and planxties, a kind of song blind harper Turlough O'Carolan wrote for his patrons. Many a modern Celt musician can thank Big Tur for his efforts, which were rescued by the great 19th-century song-collection agencies.

You'll hear stuff like this in the *seisiun* or "session," where musicians get together, often in a pub, and play their hearts out with whatever they can lay their hands on. This kind of thing, and get-togethers called *ceilis* (kay-lees), make for especially good *craic*.

## SCOTLAND

It's the land of the Scotch measure, strathspey and Highland bagpipes. The first is a kind of rhythm (as well as a drink and a dirty look), the second both a tune and dance, and the third an instrument intended to make up for the country's ongoing lack of battle strategy.

The Scots came from Irish rovers known as *Scotti* who needed more space, so sailed east to end up in a place named Dalriada, after an early Irish king. Alternative history says Milesius of the Milesians wed an Egyptian princess named Scota, who had a child called Goidel, thus Scotland and Goidelism. Others pushed north from what's now England. However it came to be, they pounded down an identity in a welter of horns, harps and hysterics.

Occasionally warring with indigenous tribe the Picts, they became so musical that one 12th-century Norman news correspondent, Giraldus Cambrensis, thought the Scots actually excelled over Ireland in music. This was in spite of the fact they got hold of the bagpipes. These figure prominently in the history of the Scottish Stuart kings, and people like 18th-century Robert Burns, a poet who periodically remained sober enough to piece together songs for us to enjoy today.

Today there are plenty of Highland pipes, small-pipes, border pipes and reel pipes, and they've all found their way into the country's rock 'n' reel musical movement. If you'd prefer, you can go for the old parlor songs like *Donald, Where's Yer Troosers?* The Scots always did like an irrational anthem.

## WALES

They may have wailed as they were pushed west over 1,000 years ago by successive waves of German-Saxons and French-Normans, but the Welsh – *Weahlas* for "foreigners," as the Saxons called them – got over it and just went on making music.

Inevitably, they came under the eye and ear of that itinerant archivist, Giraldus Cambrensis, who actually had some Welsh blood. Though he criticized his half-kin's houses, hair and the way they brushed their teeth, he had to admit they had the song-and-prophecy thing wrapped up.

One of Wales' biggest contributions to musical histtory is the grand *Eisteddfod* festival, where almost everything is unpronounceable. It almost died for all time when King Henry VIII pulled out his 1536 Act of Union to kill Welsh culture and language. The later Puritan-cum-Nonconformist religion movement also tried to shut everyone up.

In the 18th century, there was a revival in London, of all places. *The Eisteddfod* came back home, a national society was allowed to form around it, and the rest is hystery. Backing it was the long-running Welsh peculiarity of a harpers' genealogy, which has nothing to do with blood, but is more a continuity with the magical style of the old harpers. It's a certain something called *tinc,* you either have it or you don't, and it's the kind of movement that can't be obliterated.

Wales was given equality with England by the Welsh Language Act of 1973, but even before that they were learning some music from books (unlike their Irish and Scottish kith), so it's no wonder their wails are so well preserved.

## CORNWALL; ENGLAND

The Cornish are another group pushed as far west as they could go, right to the southwest cutoff point of Land's End. Their mythology is full of islands that sank eons ago, and from which, if you're lucky, you can hear watery strains of music issuing forth.

On land, Cornwall has a few good works like its *Bewnans Meriasek* (Life of St. Meriasek). It's full of musical references like "Pipers, blow quickly. We will, every son of a breast, go to dance." Thought to be the oldest surviving life of a Celtic saint in any Celtic language, it's a bright spot in a Cornish existence of getting called names, murdered, and driven to the sea. By the 1540s, these people also were told they had to speak, write and sing only in English, and then the Methodists got going on their holy cleaning sprees.

There were the inevitable stubborn holdouts, and that handy thing called "folk memory," so we do have some authentic Cornish music-and-miracle stuff left today. The Cornish *Gorsedd* High Seat festival is a gathering of bards who just can't keep quiet, because they've managed to resurrect something that died off around the 11th century. *Troyls* are musical get-togethers people took over from the trolls. And today, in amongst plenty of Cornish radical-trad stuff, there's a lot of ancient dancing. With metal-plated clog-bottoms on slate floors, you're guaranteed to make as much noise as possible. See? Definitely not "Seltic."

And as Cornwall is in England, we might as well mention that the rest of England is debatably Celtic. It did get some ancient Celts, Brigantes, who came from an old god-king named Breogan in what's now Spain, but it also is full of the descendents of invaders who drove the Celts west and north. Still, some Irish and others did come back centuries later in an immigration state of forgiveness, and put down roots music. The northeast region of Northumbria even invented its own bagpipes. The debate of England's Celticness is ongoing, but let's just say it's difficult to avoid being somewhat Celtic when you have Scotland, Ireland and Wales hemming you in, anyway.

## ISLE OF MAN

Considering it's the oldest self-governing Celtic nation in the world, it's a shame the music hasn't been better known. But that's what you get when you're small and way out off the mainland. Still, as the Manx have gone through a bewildering array of Welsh, Scandinavian and Scottish rulers, it stands to reason they got all the musical influences.

The Isle of Man has a particular body of popular sacred music, *Carvalyn Gailckagh,* which sounds like your throat does after a night of festivities. Some of these carols are over 60 verses long. It's a good thing there's anything left at all, because the same old English Only rule came to be applied here in the mid 1800s. But when you have a Scotched-up Norse legacy and are named after the Celtic ocean god Manannan Mac Lir, you find a way to get around all this.

The Manx made merry with music all right, though one of their most famous songs, *Ny Kiree fo Niaghtey*, is not exactly a go-ahead-get-happy ditty – it's about the loss of over 2,000 sheep during a bad winter storm. But sad or sassy, the Manx songs impressed the Scottish poet Burns enough to rave about them to a friend in 1794. It's not recorded how he felt about the idle piper on the island who apparently dreamed up the "Scottish" tearjerker *All Ye Banks and Braes O' Bonny Doon.* Today you'll still find some Scotch dribbled throughout the resurgence of Manx music.

## BRITTANY

Also known as Armorica – which got mixed up with "America" in various diasporas – this ancient land of

Breizh in northwest France was overrun with fifth-century Celts hot-tailing it out of Britain. Soon known as Lesser Britain, it tried to be independent, but successive waves of Vikings and Frenchmen were a real wet blanket. Breton minstrels called *conteurs* tried to keep things going.

Under the ongoing stamp of the French, Brittany simmered away until the 19th century, when it finally remembered the things it had in common with Wales, and the fact that it was, after all, Little Britain. The time was ripe for cultural revival and that included music. The Bretons also heard what was happening in Ireland. Some *ceilis* are just so boisterous they couldn't help it.

Then 19th-century Breton nobleman Hersart de Villemarque began gathering old tunes, and it's a good thing he did, because otherwise we'd have hardly any published Breton song entries. A lot of them haul in Brittany's other linguistic specialty, the Z language. You'll see this in Hersart's *Barzaz Breizh,* a big book of traditional songs and poetry from the early 1800s, and hear all about it at gatherings like the *fest-noz,* where things really drone on.

Today you'll find Breton music, with its biniou-pipes and blown-away bombardes, that blends jazzy, Bulgarian and African rhythms. We're getting closer, here, to more exotic lands like...

### CELTIC SPAIN – Galicia, Asturias:

Mix Irish beer with Spanish wine and there you are. Nauseated, maybe, but also in the region of northwest Spain that can boast a Celtic presence from 600 BCE or thereabouts. Not surprising, as much of the coastline is similar to that of Scotland, where many Celts did head to become full-flung Gaels.

The Romans muscled in around 100 CE, Germanic, Portuguese and African Moorish came to visit, and one day it was decided that Jesus' apostle St. James had been buried at Compostela. The 13th-century Galician poet Martin Codax's *Cantigas de amor and amigo* songs also upped the tourist factor. So did song-loving sailors like embattled Irish chief Red Hugh O'Donnell, who fled here after the Battle of Kinsale in Ireland, 1601. Full circle, really, as the Irish had come from Spain in the first place.

Galicians make noise with the *gaita* (bagpipe), drums and tambourines, and the *payella*, a frying pan with a long rough handle scraped with a key. The scythe is an instrument to die for, and the people love *aturuxo,* which means "screaming and shouting." From all this, you can get some picture of the liveliness of Galician music.

Dig around certain parts of Italy, Turkey and the like, and you'll also hear Celtic stuff, the fallout of Keltoi wanderings and the Internet. And, because the Celts were "Indo-European" peoples and have a lot of things in common with India, don't be surprised to get Sanskrit stuff blended amongst the bonny doons. In general, Celtic music is one big melding pot.

*

# Chapter 2

# Magic, Mythology, Meaning and Messed Up

## SUBJECTS AND PREDILECTIONS

When dawn first breaks on the stage of *Riverdance,* the only thing moving on those figures is their heads swiveling around to the back-dropped rays of dawn.

They're about to dance up a storm, literally reeling around a sun that explodes on stage. But this blessedly quiet moment of homage is noteworthy, because it represents one of the biggest things in Celtic culture. Waking up to the sun meant you had lived to see another day, and one without rain. And it was a reminder that there were great powers behind the elements.

As any of these many powers might bless or curse you, as well as assume human form, you had to try to sing, rhyme and dance their favour. All Celtic lands had variations of this, and of just about everything else mentioned in this book. And for 3,000 years, they've been making a production about it all.

As the whole culture had started off as a matriarchal one with the goddess Danu, we might as well start with the female factor. There were many goddesses, and one of the biggest was Etain, who ruled sun, water, horses, transmigration of souls and more, and was wife to sun-god-of-eloquence Ogma. She often took human form and then cloned herself: In Celtic history, you'll find more Etains than just about any other female.

The Aisling was an otherworldly figure who appeared to men in their dreams and actually represented the homeland, so she inspired any number of Odes to Erin. The Morrigan, or whatever she was called in other cultures, was a goddess who fed on both lust and death, and if you refused her advances you were doomed. The Celts are still trying to come up with the right song for this.

A hero called Dagda did mate with the Morrigan, but he also was a giant, had a magic cauldron and a harp that killed people, and didn't let much bother him. He led the Tuatha de Danaan, a crowd of warrior-gods descended from goddess Danu, all over the place, and they were so big on music Dagda would go on to practically lend his name to a musical tuning.

The Tuatha also were conduits for the *Oran Mhor* ("great music"), which was the very Energy of Creation, an idea found in many cultures. Mere mortals might aspire to at least master the three human-experience "strains" of music. *Gentraige,* the pleasant happy stuff, you might play for a family gathering, unless your family was so depressing and dysfunctional you just had to drag out the *goltraige,* melancholy music. *Suantraige* was good for the young and insomniac, as it was comforting lullaby stuff.

In Ireland, third-century *Fionn Mac CumHaill* (Finn McCool) and his kin and buddies the *Fianna* had plenty of Fenian Lays, a type of ballad celebrating the feats of the Fianna. (The word Fenian would be used centuries later as a political gimmick.) The Ossian ballads celebrate Finn's son Oisin, whose spelling was not as good as his music. There's something fishy about this whole family, though, as Finn apparently gained his wisdom from eating a magic salmon.

Animals were worshipped, humanized and hunted in equal quantities, and often connected with the Underworld and Otherworld. Magical birds trilled songs to wake the dead, and sometimes these feathered song-sters actually were humans who had been unwillingly transformed by dysfunctional deities.

If you were lucky enough to find the boar who was the symbol of the Hag of Winter, though, you could slay the beast, bring back the spring, and write a song about it. Others went for the bull and stuck the horns on their helmets, never to know Hollywood would yank them off and give them to the Vikings. The Celts spent a lot of time running around after each other's crashing boars and cattle, and the lure of a clan barbecue also inspired them. As some hoof-and-snout entrees were known to reinvent themselves over and over after being eaten, it just added to the repertoire.

This Celtic concern with livestock is seen in songs like *Maol Donn.* It laments a favourite cow that got stuck in a peat bog, and this is particularly important, because it's one origin of the bagpipes.

Amidst song cycles long enough to shame classical composer Wagner, Ireland's *Ulster Tales* introduced *Tain Bo Cuailnge,* or *The Cattle Raid of Cooley,* that in turn introduced people like the warrior-hero Chu (Ku) Chu-lainn. This bigshot didn't ride on the fact he was the son of Lugh, another sun-god, but mostly on his own dev-eloped a press-worthy "salmon-leap," a Superman-like ability to leap over anything in his path. His fame would live for centuries, all the way to a late-20th-century *Riverdance* bagpipe segment that lamented his ultimate donnfall.

Chu Chulainn is mirrored in Galicia's famous cycles about its ancient king Breogan, who managed to conquer everything around him. Breogan became such a big deal he's immortalized in the lyrics of the Galician national anthem. Wales cycled around with *The Mabinogion,* an immense work poetic enough to be Homeric. It concerned the adventures of the Mabinog, a young man trying to make it big in the bardic industry. A lot of people could identify with this, and with the way his efforts were fuelled with plenty of mead.

Some of the most passionate Celtic songwriting ever has been done around the subject of drink. The Gaelic term *uisge beatha,* which meant "water of life," came to mean whiskey. There were plenty of paeans to it, and, especially when whiskey-making was prohibited in 1790s Scotland, a torrent of dirges and laments. Today *Lament For Whiskey* and *Farewell to Whiskey* are popular in many musicians' repertoires, though no neo-Celt can perform them with the emotion that rocked the subject back then.

Manx farmers raised their mugs to the *fenodoree.* This was an ugly sprite who enjoyed helping them with their labours, so the laborers could spend more inebriated time writing water-logged musical tales about the island's sacred and tail-less cats and fish-tailed folk just off the coast. In Cornwall, fairy-like piskies and the lowly ant, thought to represent the "small people" in a state of decay, were good musical themes, but nowhere as big as giants, who were so temperamental it made for endless song material.

The Bretons sang about a bard named Hyvernion, who when he wasn't singing about them, was directed by an angel in a dream to go to Armorica to find his ideal bride. Out of this union came Saint Herve, or Harvey the Blind, a holy bard who ended up multi-tasking enough to get himself sung about for 1,500 years. Blacksmiths, spectral washerwomen and beggars-turned-bandits also were excellent theme material.

Celtic cultures simply picked up on whatever went on around them – from shape-shifting to severed heads, sassy milkmaiding and serial murderering – and wrote a song about it. There were songs to make battle, make butter, make things better, and Scottish deathbed songs in six-volume collections. The Scots always were hard workers, and have the occupational songs to prove it, but in Ireland traditionally, there were very few songs of labor. Either no one did any work or they just didn't like to sing about it.

In fact, when the Irish weren't warring they preferred to be esoteric. Their ancient *Ogham* alphabet, named after that wordy god Ogma, related each letter to a tree, so it made being called "wooden" a compliment. Select superhumans were allowed to scratch this alphabet onto stones, and it became the first rock music. Celts in general had a good grasp on language subtleties and often preferred to suggest rather than hit listeners over the head with it. This has nothing to do with the fact they often lopped off heads. That was a true sign of respect, because it was done to gain the wisdom of the enemy.

There were other ways to improve your I.Q., E.Q. or Ps and Qs, and one of the best ways to do it was to go down to the river. The significance of water flows and burbles throughout Celtic hystery and indeed that of others, like India. Rivers were connected to wisdom, life, fertility and the underworld, from the Middle Bronze Age (mid-second-millennium BCE) on. You could pick up quite a lot at the edge of the river, while crossing it at the right time and with the right rhyme could change you forever, especially if you encountered the Salmon of Knowledge along the way.

A favourite Celtic ritual was to come to the banks of a river, sing your guts out and throw in a few metalworks like weapons, armor, jewellery and coins. A precognitive sort might have said that glint of watery gold heralded one of the biggest musical moneymakers of all time a few millennia later. But a lot of things were worth doing a river dance about, right from day one.

## MAGICAL MANKIND

In Celtic days of yore, there was a lot of going back and forth between this world and the Otherworld.

Scotland's 13th-century Thomas the Rhymer is among those who got an extended trip courtesy of the Queen of Elfland. It usually was pointless to try to argue with such royalty, but you'd often return, like Thomas, a transformed human of great musical skills, all the better to sing up gods and goddesses with.

Teirtu was a Welshman who also coasted on the success of music he wasn't responsible for, and that was because his harp played itself, which instruments tended to do then. The harp of Tuatha de Danaan leader Dagda went much further one day, and leapt off the wall to slay nine Fomorri, a shape-changing tribe, then sang a paean to Dagda. Even in Celtic times, a tough act to follow.

For harper Taliesin, the real miniseries material was the story of his conception and birth. Tal, who hung around King Arthur's domain (anywhere from Cornwall to south Wales to Scotland to Brittany) originally was a kitchen boy named Gwion pursued by a witch called Ceridwen. The two kept shape-shifting themselves, until it was down to a hawk swallowing a piece of wheat. When Ceridwen settled her wings and was human again, she found she was pregnant, then simply threw this grain of truth in the ocean. The child met up with the Salmon of Knowledge and was reborn as Taliesin ("shining brow"). This reincarnation idea would become a big part of Celtic music.

Gods and goddesses were temperamental enough for endless ballad material. When Gwydyon, the Welsh god of music-and-more, was determined to possess the pigs of Pryderi, a Welsh leader, he tried to trick Pryderi with an exchange of 12 magnificent horses and 12 grey-hounds, which were mere illusions. Pryderi, cheated, came after him with a force, they had it out in single combat, and Gwydyon killed the chieftain, who promptly got sung about, and kept his pigs, which often got sung

when he lit a pascal or Easter fire on a hill overlooking the hall of Tara, to take precedence over the fire the High King himself wanted to light. The King also was a sucker for a good singer, so he listened to Pat.

St. Patrick sang all this up, and the Celts more or less listened, too. They asked whether they could retain their own "needfire," a fiery source that on one ritual night provided embers for household heads to take back to relight their own hearths. Patrick sang back that they could, as long as they didn't burn the village down doing it. He was tolerance personified and well rounded too, as he'd spent time in Egypt and other exotic parts.

Other religious were more demanding. St. Brior of Cornwall-and-Brittany accepted that chanting psalms to a pack of wolves could turn them into hairy penitents, but a pagan prince who came by and was instantly converted didn't get the same reception. Brior figured a human who could "turn" so quickly might just as quickly turn into something worse, so he set up a six-month course with exams at the end, and said take it or leave it. It shows you the power of song, though.

For Caedmon, a tone-deaf seventh-century religious student-and-cowherd, the power came during a power nap. After soaking up Bible stories from the Celtic teachers at Whitby Monastery in northeast England, he dropped off and awoke with the most marvelous paean to God and all creation. Not surprisingly, he became the feature performer at the monastery. Then, writes a famous holy man named Bede the Venerable, Caedmon took his show on the road with a Celtic harp. Another bard was born, and one with a foot in both camps.

Fulltime Celtic bards, who had a tradition of worshipping unpredictable gods and goddesses, were not immune to the Christian call, and they aimed for the top there too. Fiech, a druidic disciple and harper-singer in St. Patrick's time, went from being baptized to a bishop. He still had a soft spot for his pagan past, but now could hold his own with any Christian holy man, and this worked for his fellow Irish when they needed holy favors. Sometimes it was best to cover all bases.

Even those who didn't aim or get so high found they had certain things in common with the Christians. A lot of Gregorian, i.e., monkish, and Gaelic rhythms were similar, with equal opportunities for tapping into spirituality. St. Columbanus of the sixth century was churchly enough to compose penances for offences like stuttering in the singing of hymns, but this poet wannabe also waxed rapturous over love as a flame that had to be kindled and fed to be kept alive. It was close enough to the old Celtic needfire that kept everyone's hearts and rear ends warm.

However, there were rebels. When seventh-century Irish King Suibhne (Sweeney) discovered Bishop Ronan Finn setting up holy shop nearby, he flung a spear at the bishop's bell and found himself cursed with insanity and doomed to die at spear-point. He wandered through the forests naked and hungry for seven years before getting himself lanced by the husband of a woman who gave him milk. Sweeney died reconciled (with the Holy Sacrament), never to know his tale of woe would be musically embraced by mega-production *Riverdance* as its eeriest segment, *Shivna*. It has a nice Indo-European parallel with the Hindu god Shiva, who stands for the death and destruction of bad habits.

Whatever they thought about the influx of Christianity (Celtic, or the more oppressive Roman blazing in after the 600s), the Celts have the monks to thank for writing down their ancient sagas, which really is what saved Ireland in the end. That stubborn Celtic insistence on trained memory just took its toll after a while. So, out came the holy songbooks. Some bards were brought in to monasteries as inhouse historians and genealogists to help it along.

Even as Christianity became increasingly Romanized, priests and bishops kept their ears peeled for poets' offerings they thought they could adapt for their brethren. Some of these Anglo-Irish numbers were good enough to get into the Latin hymnals. If the natives ever felt they'd sold out, welcome to the publishing industry.

Still, they still were allowed to use their harps to accompany their words, while clerics had their own harps, a handy little eight-string number with the name of *oct-tedact,* they wore suspended from their girdles. This left their hands free for any number of other things, like occasional simony to accompany the hymnony.

A lot of monks, like the ninth-century Culdees, were extremely well-travelled. The Culdees were a Celto-Saxon musical monastic order who brought influences from the Middle East, even that hotspot Jerusalem, to add to the ecumenical flavour Celtic Christianity already had. Even today some scholars say certain Celtic chant has a Hebraic flavour, others that West Highland psalm-singing echoes Middle Eastern and Ethiopian chants, and is really what's behind North American bluegrass music. It's obvious the Celts still intended to take over the world.

These elements enhanced a new Christian religion that had its foundation in the spaced-out spirituality already strong in Ireland and Scotland. The missionaries realized the value of keeping their new flocks happy with enough of the something old, something familiar, even if they drew the line at Egyptian worship, a favourite Celtic hobby. That only started because Osiris got confused with Oisin, but it was something to keep an eye on.

Most of the mass was sung, which was a selling point to convertees, and many hymns used for liturgy's sake had a reassuring pagan character. There was the belief in general that hymn singing gave magical immunity against fire, poison and wild animals, a good way to up dwindling church attendance. There also were crafty offerings like *The Loves of Taliesin* (that fish-brained bard of King Arthur's time). This Welsh work actually is a holy chant all about penance, but its tabloid title certainly reeled them in.

The Church also did it *en mass* with Antiphonaries, books of church music meant to be sung back and forth between two people, a kind of "call and response" act, evident in later Celtic times, that let the public get involved. There also were hymns for the Trinity-cum-shamrock in three-part hymnony, and for the Virgin Mary. One of the biggest here was a 148-verse effort composed by one of the O'Dalys, that axe-happy Irish clan that obviously had an even gentler artistic side.

Overall, the Celts could identify Mary with their ancestral goddesses, especially with one diverse goddess who also morphed into the Irish St. Brigid. The Hebridean Islanders in Scotland were strong on Brigid, who in an earlier incarnation had attended the "Mother of Naza-reth," and didn't find it beneath her to tend island mums in their crofts.

When Brigid wasn't easing labor pains, she labor-ed away as the patron saint of music, as well as of poetry and learning. And as her father was the famous Fiech, that druid-harper who achieved the hilltop of the new religion, she had a support system in place for some years. A seventh-century hymn to Brigid tells us she also was ordained as a bishop by St. Patrick's nephew Mel. Yet another entry for a CV that already included triune goddess, midwife and mother figure in general.

To spread the Word, it helped if you knew something about PR, and Brittany's sixth-century Saint Herve cert-ainly did. Being born sightless was a start, because it so often heralded the beginning of a good Celtic musician, but Herve had a likeable face, a sweet voice, the golden harp of his father Hyvernion, who had been a royal minstrel, and the song output of both his parents, which was considerable.

He took all of this, as well as a companion wolf, out on the road to conversion with him, and it all worked in his favour when he ultimately became an abbot. Because he'd journeyed so far to do it, he also became the patron saint of travelling musicians as well as of bards in general.

Breton "Patron" or Pardon days began to spring up around local saints and holy relics. There were processional prayers and penances to commemorate the day, but inevitably it would become a fair, with music, dancing and a few bawdy miracles thrown in. In keeping with that age-old idea of the gods being a down-to-earth breed, natives believed the deities were there in more than spirit. And in spite of the fact things sometimes ended in fisticuffs over a wooden statue (the kind of token thought to bring better crops) these big P days generally were happy affairs.

In Brittany, they also sang the praises of *Saint-Jean-du-Doigt*. In a medieval age when relics abounded, John the Baptist's finger was one of the best. A French traveling salesman brought it to town, and it was such a mommentous thing the church bells began making merry of their own accord. Any time the peasants got revolting, the church bigwig just showed them the finger and they sang respectfully to it.

Brittany also is famous for its musical triplets named Guenole, Venec, and Jacut, all of whom become saints. The trio's first big hit was singing the praises of their mother, St. Given, who had grown a third mammary gland to cope with the birth disorder, and from then on they kept abreast of what the public wanted, within certain sacred dictates.

It was this kind of Celtic versatility that also made music like Cornwall's carols appropriate for both

Christian and pagan celebrations, while Brittany seconded the notion with its equally versatile *kantik.* The throat-clearing *Carvalyn Gailckagh,* that body of sacred tales and music embraced by men and women of The Isle of Man, got a lot of its material from the Manx Bible. Because these people were away out on an island, they'd been allowed to make their own, and they did it with some Norse and Scotch thrown in.

But as time went on, a lot of holy men came down really hard on native music, regarding it as the work of the devil. Many Celts paid lip service to this, then on Saturday nights locked the doors tight (so the devil couldn't get away) and whooped, hollered, blew and made merry. Any lingering doubts could be exorcised away in church next day. There was the odd music-loving priest who played the fiddle. But the 18th-century Methodist and Non-Conformist church crowd, in particular, did their best to stamp out the merrymaking.

Then, just as a few hundred years before, some of them actually began working native rhythms into the Sunday school curriculum. These were infectious times. Even the really rigid hellfire-and-damnation lot had their own "if you can't beat 'em, join 'em" tactic, a sacred music called *hwyll.* A semi-chant they used in preaching, it was close enough to singing to seduce the music-loving Welsh.

Creating melodies for the common people was one of the best ways to reach them, as Rev. James MacGregor found. Jimmy, who came from the Scottish Highlands to Nova Scotia, Canada, in 1786, as the first Gaelic-speaking Protestant minister in that province, slapped some happy tunes on the Gaelic Calvinist-religious poetry he wrote, and even went so far as to compose some real crowd-pleasers on secular themes like earthly love and anti-slavery.

Alexander Carmichael opted out of the Nova Scotia run because he had enough to do at home in Scotland.

Carmichael, who was born in 1832, and like a good Celt didn't get weighed down with formal academic training, devoted years to putting together an exhausting, multi-volume Scottish Gaelic collection known as the *Carmina Gadelica.* Filled with poems, prayers, hymns, chants and songs laced with some Druidism and other diversities, it was a welcome recognition of a spiritual heritage that had been doing a song and dance for some time.

Alex may not have made it to the New World, but his efforts certainly did. The C.G. gave Gaelic settlers lots of material to draw from, any time they felt they'd been shipwrecked from their spirituality. And in the 1990s, Nova Scotia composer Scott Macmillan would embrace this Celtic-Christian epic, along with other works, to write his *Celtic Mass for the Sea,* for orchestra, Celtic ensemble and full choir. You'd think such Gael-force treatment would blow this gentle spirituality away, but sometimes the ninth, 12th or 19th century needs a boost.

Modern Celtic Christian music gives us any number of progressive spiritual bands who sing up ancient pray ers for St. Columba, St. Patrick and his breastplate, mystical holy places like Iona and Lindisfarne, and other saints like Columcille, Cuthbert, Aidan and Addendum.

This kind of music reflects a new-old movement religious scholars are still arguing about. But Celtic Christianity, which took pride in distancing itself from the more oppressive Roman Christianity, always was strong on nature, magic, male-female equality and general overall respect. There are worse things to sing up in religion.

# Chapter 4

## Instrumental Voices

When Polybius, Diodorus, and the rest of the early Greek news anchors documented the Celts, they had plenty to say about their voices. Yes, out of the mouths of Keltoi came some frightening stuff.

If Polybius and his crew could have followed the Celts through their coming-of-age in Ireland, Scotland and beyond, they would have had lots more to report, like about how complex and refined the whole Celtic musical thing became. Wild and spirited, yes, but also highly literary, allusive, ornamented and splitting off after a while into a bewildering variety of vocal applications.

One of the first known kinds of Celtic singing was what Finn McCool, his son Oisin and all their warriors back in the third century did to amuse themselves when they weren't warring or making up tall tales. They jammed their lips together and made bagpipe sounds. Even if some primitive form of the pipes existed then, this was the great equalizer, a way for everyone to drone on together.

That wasn't all Finn and his crew did in the way of song. Their Fenian Lays, set usually in stanzas or four-line verses, each line with seven syllables, were considered just about the best thing a Gael could sing. These lays celebrated various earthly and unearthly feats, from slaying giants to getting slain by giant curses. Finn was big enough a man not to mind a laugh at his expense, and one of the best of the lays described the time he got trapped in a castle, singing all the way.

About the oldest surviving kind of Irish singing done with mouths open is *sean-nos*. It means "old-style," and the second word is pronounced "nose," as it's a terribly nasal kind of thing. It seems to have worked well for bards, but for listeners today, it's something to come to grips with.

Apart from having some parallels in the trad singing of other cultures, like Arabic, singers throw in different dialects, use all sorts of rolls and differences in timbre and stress, slap several notes on each syllable and come to abrupt stops. There's none of the loud-and-soft of more classical music, but enough melody variations verse to verse to make you wish for a good old *geis*.

Ireland also is known for something called the macaronic song, a stew of half-English, half-Irish lyrics, often with rhymed vowels. You'd hear it aplenty at the time of the English-Irish takeover, which was often enough. You'll also hear it in *Lord of the Dance,* in which a goddess named Erin sings a song called *Suil a Ruin.* As it has slightly different spellings, people still argue about what the title means, but it's pronounced "Shool Aroon," and the whole thing seems to be a lament for a lover who fled martial oppression to join a foreign army. These flighty types were known as Wild Geese, and it all made for a lot of honking and squawking.

The Celts also perfected a high art of sung satirical verses and incantations that could turn the rivers dry, cause death or, even worse, make pimples sprout on your face. Irish insults were known as *aels* and *aers,* and the Scots had satirical *flytings,* rife with rhymes and alliteration that could get downright nasty. Sticks and stones were one thing, but these words could really hurt you. They were weapons, as much as sword, spear and bagpipes had been from the start.

Besides being flighty, and letting rip with churchly psalm singing, the Scots hit it big with *puirt-a-beul* ("poorsht a beel"). It's also called "mouth music" or lilting or jigging, and they have it in Ireland too. It was done to imitate the sounds of seals, birds and bagpipes, to mourn the dead, and to provide dance rhythms.

Mouth music is full of words or sounds that sound simply nonsensical. In fact, it can become so complex you'd think they were singing in code, and often they were. Periodically, Church and State came down hard on music-makers and lyrics, but here was one instrument, the indecipherable human voice, they couldn't destroy (they'd stopped cutting out tongues by the age of gunpowder because it was considered barbaric).

*Caoineadh* was simply lamentable. Or simply a lament. In many places it was a female tradition, of coming in to "keen" the deceased with lots of high-pitched wailing. As the theme of the singing was based on the life of the person who had died, it was a way to pay tribute and to achieve some kind of closure. The keener might even take on the persona of the deceased, an early example of having your identity stolen, though it's doubtful the victim much cared. This idea was taken to an especially high art in Wales, but really is hysterical enough to be found in any Celtic culture.

*Canntaireachd,* on the other hand, is a traditional kind of chanted music designed to help teach students about the unforgiving quality of the Highland bagpipes, and their special music, *piobaireachd* (just say "pibroch"). Those who are totally unforgiving about anything to do with the bagpipes might feel the same about this vocal stuff, but they should at least admire the Scots for their ingenuity in getting around the no-notation dilemma for this so-called classical music form.

Everyday Celtic voice got a good workout in epic songs, which went on and on about everything including the kitchen drunk. Ballads also were big, but tended to be about a single thing, like an episode of incest, death or worse, with lots of repetition. Another kind of ballad was called the *muckle sang* – and as it often had to do with important battles, you had to be careful not to muck things up. An oral culture depended on it.

There was a particularly laborious type of Scottish ballad created by job-seeking farmhands at summer fairs. As they traded stories on the tough rural life and red flags against undesirable employers, it all got put into song, along with some locker-room stuff. This whole body of dust and lust was called the *cornkister* or bothy ballad, "bothy" being a migrant worker's hut. Sometimes the whole thing became too bothersome, and the lads would head for any body of water they could find to immerse themselves in a few *jorram,* or rowing songs.

Another occupational offering was the *waulking* song, which has nothing to do with the feet, but a lot to do with the hands. A whole crew crowds around a long table to work, tumble and torture raw wool that's been soaked with urine, an age-old Celtic household staple. The cloth is consecrated by a woman leader, then each member whom the wool will garb is brought out in prayer, and everyone wails away, rocking back and forth over their labors.

Also called a milling frolic, this primitive variation of the quilting bee was a chance to exchange all the gossip, which usually was far too salty to be consecrated. You still might stumble upon the occasional walking-milling scenario in Scotland and Cape Breton, Canada, and if so, you've been warned.

Another ceremony that has alarmed from-away bystanders is the Breton *Kan ha Diskan,* or call-and-response singing. Two people alternate chants, then join together at the end, and sometimes several pairs go at it at once. What these people are doing is not duets. It's more a matter of two separate entities trying to get along with and outdo each other. In any case, when they get tired of not being a duet (and many do), they can do a nice simple *gwerz,* or ballad.

But in fact a lot of *gwerziou,* the whole Breton tradition of solo unaccompanied singing, has themes that are really frightening, worse than anything you'll find on late-knight TV. For light relief, there are the *sonniou* songs, that do their best not to upset anyone, even as they keep the culture alive. Still, Bretons are inclined to mix the sacred and profane, the heavenly and hellish, on one recording, and it's quite something to hear, if you understand the P and Z languages.

Bretons like to do things by the letter, and nowhere is this more apparent than in a Seven Years War incident in 1758, when the British attacked St. Malo. Some of the Brits were Welsh who sang all the way over and didn't stop as they waded ashore. The Bretons recognized these songs as some of those P language ditties common to both lands, embraced their linguistic cousins, and disaster was averted. Many historians dispute this version, but the power of song throughout Celtic history is strong enough that you might as well disregard such naysayers.

One of the oldest Galician vocal traditions is called the *Riveiranas,* done in strange musical codes to prevent anyone else from horning in. It's one thing that's enabled the Galicians to keep their national identity, which really is a mishmash of that multicultural tourist trade that got going from 100 CE on. Galician *alalas* are chants based on a single theme that just drone on, with or without Galician bagpipes, and that sound Celtic enough, but also are spiced with that Germanic and Arabian seasoning from centuries ago.

Other pundits claim *alalas* are patterned after the Phoenician rowing songs *alelohuias,* while still others go for a Greek basis. The whole thing evokes a hypnotic effect similar to that of Gregorian chant. In fact, many Galicians were so impressed with what they heard wafting over the monastery walls they decided to take it and rework it for their own use. The whole *alalas* thing became over time a point of much patriotic pride – though you could always take time out to do sexy love stuff like the *habaneras* songs – and it was jealously protected from the Spanish, who periodically horned in. Overall, Galician singing did suffer under 20th-century Francesco Franco, but even the mightiest dictator can't really take the music away from the people.

Any lingering resentment could be worked out in the Galician song duel known as the *desafío*. It's a part-icularly virulent kind of call-and-response act, in which groups of women scream insults at each other. There are a lot of barnyard references here, and the whole thing makes you sorry for anyone who might get in their way.

The Welsh, now – well, you'd really have to go to a millennium-long Eisteddfod to take it all in. There's just so much going on there, and it goes way back. In early days bards made their mark with an incredibly complex system of musical alliteration. It was called *cynghanedd,* it means roughly "harmony,"and it's unique to Wales because no one else wanted to do it.

*Penillion,* a part of *cynghanedd,* involved a singer trying to keep pace with a bardic harper, who would mix and mash meter, measure and other musical aspects at his whim. It could be happy or sappy, fast or slow. While the singer didn't have to begin with the harper, he did have to end precisely with him, so it's a specialized thing. Other pairs do back-and-forth songs, another thing the Welsh have in common with the Bretons.

*Plygain,* a musical melee at cock crow, or early morning, Christmas mass, basically involves trying to outsing your neighbours and certainly any outsiders.

41

The words to each song were copyrighted, even if it took a weapon or druid to do it, within families. The Welsh have proved a little looser with the songs they sang and still sing for driving the cattle and other oxymorons. Like most Celts, they've had a strong enough bond with animals to include them in the Welsh specialty of "singing funerals." It's really music to die for, at least in quantity, as it starts at the house or barn, continues to the church, and ends at the grave.

Wales, which often was suppressed by a heavy Church hand, somehow has become known for its churchly singing. Hymns, especially in choirs, tend to be sung in four-party harmony. This is an exception in the Celtic arena of melody-only, and it's because the Welsh are geographically smaller than their Irish-Scottish non-cousins that they felt they had to make up for it. There's also plenty of Welsh chapel-singing in Patagonia, South America, where many *Weahlas* went in the 1800s.

Wales is especially known for its male choirs, called *cor meibion.* Men did whatever they could to keep their spirits up in the mining industry, so one industry begat another. These deep-down ditties also had a place in Celtic Iberia, which should tell you something about industry there.

As for otherworldly singing, a lot of people heard it and a lot of people, like Thomas the Rhymer, also got it. All along, it was considered desirable to be given some musical instruction from the other side as long as you didn't become impossible with it, and acceptable to be shown a few vocal tricks by human old-timers. But it seems there's nothing as disastrous to a good traditional voice as some classical training.

The 19th-century scholar Dr. Richard Henebry had a lot to say about this in his 1928 *Handbook of Irish Music.* Not only did he sneer about children being taught "the modern scale," but he swore he "had known" some really nifty traditional singers. Their success had prompted them to take "lessons in voice production from common modern teachers." After that, it seemed, they just couldn't sing properly anymore because they'd had the mickey taken right out of them.

Soprano, alto and bass have no place in traditional music. You sing whatever pitch you prefer that day. The overall unschooled quality of Celtic music would travel across the Atlantic in later years, to become the "high lonesome" sound of North American country music. This characteristic may have had a lot to do with sheer homesickness. The Welsh call these feelings of longing *hiraeth,* and it's one of those things that defies an exact translation. If you feel it, you know it.

\*

## Chapter 5

# Carrying That Tune

## THE RHYTHM METHOD

Many thought the ancient Celts to be simply noisy, but in fact their music early on had both rhyme and reason to it. According to 19th-century English scholar Matthew Arnold, rhyme is a direct legacy of the Celts, and the greeting card industry thanks them for it. But more than that, it was part of the "reason" that ruled the ancient Celtic world.

Meter was important, and nowhere is this more apparent than in a famous justice scenario in ancient Ireland. An *ollave* or bigshot poet ticked off at a king who he felt hadn't given him a big enough reward, would go to a hilltop at dawn. He would sing a stanza in a certain meter, then put some stones and thorns at the butt of a hawthorn tree. If the poet was in the wrong, the earth would swallow him; if the King had erred, he and his kin got consumed. This shows plenty of self-confidence, as well as where that saying about sticks and stones got a bit confused.

Celtic music on the whole is pretty even-tempered, from 2/4 (two beats to a measure, the quarter note gets beat), to 6/8 and 12/8. But then you get music that brings in Eastern-European rhythms like 9/16, which can't be described at all. These things can disturb you if you're used to more "regular" one-and-two-and-three-and-four rhythms, but it had to happen. The Celts, after all, were doing their thing all over Europe, so it's only right they took some Continental measures.

Brittany itself has some ill-timed affairs. A well-known Breton piece, *Wedding Tune*, goes back and forth from 3/4 to 2/4, throws in some 5/4 toward the end, and closes back at 2/4, so you can only imagine what the honeymoon was like. The Breton Christmas carol, *Peh Trouz 'Zou ar en Doar* (What Noise on Earth?) zooms from 9/8 to 15/8 and 12/8, then back again. As most Breton music comes from its pipers anyway, this is yet another reason to be wary of bagpipes.

## MULTICULTURAL MEASURES

Celts like diatonic or diabolic scales of seven tones and half tones. If they don't have time for that, they'll do a pentatonic scale of five tones to the octave, which is found also in Chinese music.

If this seems offbeat, consider that around 800 BCE, some Celts spread out across the Asian wilderness as far as China, and helped get the Iron Age going out there. Stands to reason when you're instituting an important era you'll relax with a little common music. Even Japanese songs like *Sakura* and *Sukiyaki* have found their way into Celtic harpers' repertories.

That's just the beginning. A lot of Celtic rhythms are similar to those of Polynesia, Africa, the Middle East and indigenous America. India has scales called *ragas* that can blend with some Irishness, and that common Indo-European root of both cultures can be blamed for this. Both are strong on melody and rhythm as opposed to harmony, and music from a divine source. Both drone on with instruments, like the Irish uillean bagpipes and Indian stringed tambura, with one monotonous note that got grounded long ago and never found its way back.

The mordent, a kind of sad wandering from one note to the next and back again wandered over from Byzantine Europe. The language rhythms of Romany gypsies, who did Ireland, and the Sanskrit languages of north India, also mesh so you can see some lyric potential there.

Some historians claim Welsh and Irish are tied in with the Egyptian and Berber Hamitic languages of North Africa, and Semitic tongues like Hebrew, as well as with Mycenaean Greek – and if so, things couldn't be more multiCeltural.

The Greek aspect is important, because it's where the modes, seven different progressions of diatonic scales, come from. It was philosopher-mathematician-music maven Pythagoras in the sixth and fifth centuries BCE, who set them for all time. Each mode corresponded to a heavenly body, and were thought to differently affect ordinary human body and mind. Keltoi druids and mystics came across the modes in Greece, as well as in Babylonia and Egypt, and brought them home.

Lots of Celtic music can be found in the major-sounding Ionian mode; the Mixolydian which tries to be major but flats out on the seventh note; the Dorian and the distressed Aeolian. The Phrygian mode tends to sound Spanish-Moorish, so it's big in Galician and Asturian music.

As for the Locrian, it's called the devil's mode, and it's too diabolic to have any music written in it. It's partially responsible for the whole modal thing being supplanted by our modern major and minor scales by around 1500 CE. However, the modes, like magical mankind pushed underground, were only down but not out. They would haunt the world and keep the old music alive.

## REAL REELS

Reels, jigs, double jigs, slip jigs, slop jugs, strathspeys and Scotch snaps, marches, and music that puts on plenty of airs – this, and more, is Celtic music.

The reel, which usually is in 4/4 time, comes from the Anglo-Saxon *rulla* ("to whirl") or Norse-Gaelic *ruidhle* or *righil* ("dancing and capering"), and that's not surprising. A lot of Celts were left reeling in the south of Britain when the Germanic Saxons invaded around 400

AD. The Norse muscled in later with their little thrust-and-harry sword dances.

Reels, which show up in the earliest bagpipe collections, were popular for Celtic get-togethers, and would hit the hoedown circuit in America centuries later. Those fiddlers would develop a syncopated way (of stressing out a beat that's weak to begin with) of playing reels some called sink-or-swim. A lot of old reels have disturbing names *like The Ranting Widow* and *The Flogging Ball.*

As for the jig, Shakespeare was so ill-taken with the Scottish version he called it a "hot and hasty measure." From the Italian *gigue*, it's usually in an "8" timing of 6/8, 9/8 or 12/8, and comes in singles, doubles, slips and slops. The jig idea has slopped over into other Celtic cultures, though the Galician-Asturian traditional 6/8 *muineira* dance is looser and swingier than its Scottish-Irish counterpart. It has a more free-wheeling bar pattern and fewer notes to trip you up, and it may leave you in a better mood the morning after, all the better to do a nice 2/4 *alborada* to bring up the sun.

But even the march rhythm, used for armies setting off to war, could trip you up because speeded-up marches tended to become double jigs. Fast or slow, marches often were frowned upon by the authorities not at the helm of that battle. They considered these rhythms in-citeful rather than insightful, and often blamed them for sedition.

The Strathspey, named for the *strath* or valley of the Highlands' Spey River, is a peculiarly Scottish tune-and-dance that's been blamed for a lot of things, because it's got strange little rhythms all over the place, and something called the Scotch Snap, where the fiddler "snaps" his bow quickly to get a nice jagged sound. The Scotch measure is an older type of rhythm that usually got going with a generous pour into one's mug, raised or not to capricious spirits.

Some ingenious Celt drinking from a horn one day then attached it to a wooden pipe, and the hornpipe – instrument, rhythm and dance – was born. Those who got hold of French wine welcomed the quadrille, a square-dance forerunner done by Napoleon's crowd in 19th-century France. The polka hit the Celtic arena as revenge from eastern Europe. And the mazurkas, rhumbas and fandangos that wormed their way into Galician and Asturian music come from Spanish oppressors who did know how to throw a party.

If by now you need something a little more relaxing, there's always the *Fionn Mall,* a slow Gaelic air. Airs in general are all the tunes that don't fit into any other category, and many Celtic musicians have become big by putting on lots of them.

## INEQUALS AND INEGALS

The basic idea in Celtic music and especially in dance tunes is a melody of four or eight measures, repeated once, followed by an equal-length relative melody, also repeated. This sounds simple enough.

But then that single melody line gets decorated up to the nth degree, with things like rolls and cuts, slurs (as insulting as *aels* and *aers*), trills, triplets (three notes that think they're twins), grace notes, dotted-rhythms, and other dotty variations.

So, learning the melody, as well as forgetting about harmony, is just the beginning in playing traditional music. And don't look for stuff like crescendo and diminuendo or, necessarily, the grand conclusion most high-falutin' classical music is brought to. To some dual-camp musicians, there are occasional parallels, like the Baroque music "swing" called *inegal,* which mirrors a certain lilt in Irish music. But on the whole, getting into Celtic music is a dangerously circular kind of thing, in and out and back again, like those Celtic designs with loopy embellishment that never ends.

Assuming you don't get trapped forever in a body of music, one of the most important things to remember is to never play a tune the same way twice, even when sober. Get a group of musicians together, and you'll see they all have their own way of doing it, anyway.

Ironically, some of the most advanced courses in Celtic music today have to do with "learning improvisation." This would be essential for classical musicians who'd like to switch allegiances – if they can stop thinking traditional musicians are out of tune. But it's maybe also an important kind of education for anyone who didn't grow up in a Gaelic musical household.

## MORE DANCING AND PRANCING

For 3,000 years, the Celts have been kicking up their heels to some beat or other. They did it to worship trees and booze, to prepare for wars, work, courtship, and generally let off steam.

When the Normans came to places like Ireland in the 12th century, they periodically stopped stamping on natives long enough to introduce delights like the "carol" dance, with a hyper singer in the centre, and dancers stomping around him throwing the song back at him. This partly was to keep warm in a cold, damp climate. The environment also was responsible, by the 1500s, for competitive dances like The Hey, which involved partners getting all twisted up together, and another dance that involved groups of people fighting over a handkerchief.

The Scots took your basic reel rhythm to come up with a particularly energetic version, the Highland Fling. In spite of its name, it's a disciplined thing, because it was ancient warriors dancing on a small round shield called a *targe,* with a sharp spike of steel in its center, who set the standard here. Scotland also has sword dances, as do most Celtic lands. The Isle of Man's smaller scale resulted in a dirk dance, done traditionally to get to the throne. A lot of contenders have become quite crossed trying.

Galicia crossed gym glass with traditional rhythms to come up with dancing that is athletic, to say the least – at least, in the southern part of the province. The higher up you go geographically, the lower the arms are held in dancing. Brittany went even lower; when the cattle started lowing, the cowherds created diverse stamping dances to keep the wolves at bay. Bretons also began to do it in all sorts of line and round formations they claim are much more user-friendly than what the Scottish and Irish came up with.

This brings us to the step dance, about the biggest thing in the whole arena of Celtic dance. Eighteenth century travelling Irish dance masters clacked around the countryside on silver-buckled shoes to teach the various complicated steps. The social enjoyment of the whole thing did bring down the wrath of Church and State by the 19th century, but the Gaelic League was allowed to form to promote cultural awareness. Other Celtic lands, like Galicia, did the same thing.

But then things get pretty mixed up. Crossroads dancing and house parties got closed down. People were allowed to dance in a parish hall, under the beady eye of the village priest. But then group dancing overall got stamped on, because it made for too much body contact. Make it solo performance only, insisted the powers-that-be.

Irish step dancing, especially at festivals called *feisanna*, is all bound up with standards like "points crossed feet" and "up the back," which really refers to the steel rod everyone gets fitted with. The upper body and arms are rigid as rigor mortis, the legs go like pistons or rubbery pretzels, and the feet stamp and clatter away in special shoes with frightening fiberglass, steel or composite tips and heels, except when it's a soft-shoe dance. You learn specific dances to recorded music whose tempo has been altered a bit, which is why a lot of Irish dancers can't dance to live bands. And if you want to have any hope of competing, you start dancing at around age three.

You also learn to wear garish dresses so stiff with embroidery they stand up by themselves, and expensive enough to put your parents in the poorhouse. The idea that this garb, along with kinky wigs and tiaras, represents "Irish peasant dress" of a few hundred years ago doesn't really hold water.

In any case, the whole "my elaboration is better than yours" overkill would get the heave-ho in the mid-1990s with the producers of *Riverdance,* and its music would make you forget there ever had been such an excess.

*

# Chapter 6

# MultiCeltural Instruments:
## Bagpipes and Byblows

If you take a good look at the *Riverdance* orchestra or just your atypical Celtic band, you'll discover it's full of French, Italian, German, Turkish, African, American, Greek and grotesque instruments. The loudest of them, bagpipes and other low blows, insisted on having their way first, and there's little point in arguing with these aerophones, as scholars call them.

About the earliest Celtic instruments that sounded off in a big way were the Bronze Age horn, usually yanked right off the head of the entrée, and one particularly fearsome noisemaker called the carnyx. This was long, made of beaten-up bronze and blown vertically, which meant the sound could travel on waves above its holder. It might even have a carved boar's head with moveable tongue and jaw. Greek historian Polybius also gushed about Celtic trumpet playing at the Battle of Telemon in 225 BCE. Their blowing was every bit as awesome as their blows, he said.

But even these impressive offerings got drowned out by the bagpipes on the lung-and-winding road of Celtic music history. Scotland makes the most noise about them, and part of it has to do with the 5,000-year-old archeological excavations in Sumeria (ancient Iraq) that brought up evidence of a pipester with kilt, sporran and feathered bonnet.

The ancient Spartans also had a thing for solo pipe-playing contests, and some of them really droned on. This is because pipes had a reed or two whose note never changes, an arguably lazy idea that would translate into one of the biggest things in Celtic music.

Ancient Egyptian and Babylonian royalty had pipes, and the bag first appeared in a primitive form around 1300 BCE, though went in and out of fashion after that. As the bag also was called a chorus, things often got confusing and noisy. The chanter, the part you blow, was inserted right into it like a big meat tester, courtesy of some music-loving diner.

Greek poet Homer chats about pipes. And they were so big in ancient Rome that when the pipers used for circuses, banquets and state occasions went on strike, it almost was the fall of Rome. Though some kind of damage control was worked out, the crisis left such an impression that a few hundred years later, historians were still talking about it. Some wandering Celts heard the whole thing and stored it away in their boars' heads.

In any case, when the Romans invaded Britain around 55 BCE, the Celts had pipes to outdo them, which is one reason the Romans weren't successful. Occasionally the Celtic defenders would play out of tune. Throughout the Middle Ages from 450 CE on, the pipes continued to punch up battles, football games and picnics.

The whole idea also split off into various Celtic regionalities. Wales began to make merry with the *pibacwd* and the *pibgorn*, a backwards kind of hornpipe and part of a far-flung family ranging from Ceylon to Greece to Scandinavia. Cornwall was in two minds about the whole thing, and came up with bagpipes stuck with a pair of chanters of different lengths.

The Bretons have their *biniou*, which often gets teamed with another alarming blown instrument called the *bombarde*. This is a useful arrangement as it it means one player can cover for another if he runs out of wind. The *biniou-braz* and *veuze* are bigger Breton pipes, while the Galicians and Asturians have different versions of something called the *gaita*, an old word for a watchman who'd horn in to raise the alarm. The gaita is alarming enough, strident enough to make the fillings in your teeth jump out.

None of these pipes can compete with the Scottish Highland version. However the pipes got to Scotland, they immediately took on a starring role that has lasted to this day. They were good for war, noisy in peacetime, and also had their own superstars, most notably members of the great MacCrimmon clan. Whether or not the MacCrimmons descended from a harper called Cremona in Italy – a point in favour of the argument that the harp influenced bagpipe music – here was a family who really bagged this instrument.

As well as being hereditary pipers of the Lairds of MacLeod, they ran a piping college that opened with a flourish-and-a-skirl around 1500 on the Isle of Skye. And in it, no one was allowed to taint the air with any of that *ceol* ("kyol") *beag*, or small music: It spoiled one's taste and ability for the major pipe stuff, the *ceolmhor,* a big body of music you might call classical, for want of a better word. Part of it, the Highland pipes'special music, *piobaireachd,* really was put up on a pedestal.

The MacCrimmons also thought so highly of themselves that when one of them went into battle and might die, he wrote his own piped lament, because there was no one else worthy of it. The family did occasionally have to moonlight, by driving herds of cattle from the Highlands to lowland markets, and this is considered a low drone in their history. But as one of them had been given a silver pipe chanter by the Queen of the Fairies, the MacCrimmons generally were respected.

The Irish have their own remarkable pipe players, but nothing is as remarkable as what those ancient Irish warriors did to relax and rejuvenate themselves, with their lips jammed together. By Finn McCool's time, it was made by as many as 50 men droning in concert. Eventually, this took so much out of them they decided to forget about doing it by mouth, which is why we mostly associate the *uillean* or "elbow" bellows-driven pipe with Ireland.

These really came into the consciousness of the world-at-large with *Riverdance*. Right from its first full-length show in 1995, it has featured an instrumental solo lamenting the mythical Irish hero Chu Chulainn. A lone figure sits, strapped into a brace-like contraption that gets fingered and squeezed to plaintive effect. And though the uillean pipes are not as frightening as their Highland cousin, they do have a certain effect on the unwary. More than one listener has likened their sound to a high lonesome cow, and the whole thing looks like a milking event anyway. This was done to commemorate the cow stuck in mud who started the whole idea.

One of the most intriguing international entries is the *duda,* the Hungarian bagpipe with a goat's head chanter, and which for some reason was rescued from near distinction by classical composers Zoltán Kodály and Béla Bartók. Look for bagpipes, too, in just about any of the other lands the ancient Celts deflowered and defamed, from Poland to Macedonia to Sicily. The most multicultural pipes of all may be the *Eryri* pipes, made by Goat Industries in North Wales, that manage to combine Scottish, Irish, Hungarian and Bulgarian ideas.

But the tiny country of Luxembourg has a weirder ace up its chanter with popular modern musical performer Cyberpiper, who took midi bagpipes, a groove-box and voice transformer and simply went techno to bard out against planetary injustice. And yes, the Keltoi were in Luxembourg at one time, except that at that time it wasn't even known as something that comes between Germany and Belgium.

As for the amiable-looking Albrecht Dürer-created character on the front of this book, he supposedly was an Irish piper in the employ of English King Henry VIII. Henry loved pipers when he wasn't banishing them from the kingdom, and was quite a piper himself. He'd been destined for the Church before the heir-apparent older brother died, and learning music was a part of a holier-than-thou career. At the time of his death, an inventory of Henry's 300 musical instruments included five sets of bagpipes, and not just any old. We're talking "ivorie" and "purple vellat" here.

But even if you were a musically challenged drone, you might get some otherworldly help, like the piper in Ireland who found himself yanked off to an otherworldly feast, where the inhabitants stopped moaning long enough to ask him to entertain that evening. He did, and found to his surprise he was playing all sorts of stuff. By the time they dumped him back at the bridge with a new set of pipes, he'd been transformed into the best piper in Ireland.

This sort of thing happened even more than with harps, because fairies and other fey folk figured if they couldn't beat the pipes, they could only try to help the pipers.

As time went on, some pipes left Ireland and Scotland to cross the Atlantic, and those that weren't thrown overboard blared out an improv fanfare for the New World. Certainly, the pipes awed the native Indian tribes. They knew all about big birds and their use at the dinner table, but they'd never thought of taking a goose and blowing on its head long enough to get an entire body of so-called music out of it.

The general adherence of Canada to the bagpipes is enough to put Scotland to shame. Partly because of geographical isolation, Gaelic settlers in Nova Scotia were determined to keep the traditional way of learning going strong. This involved that strange kind of mouth music called *canntaireachd*, using Gaelic singing that's more garbled than usual to teach the bagpipe tunes. Add this to the list that already includes the Fianna humdingers and an unhappy cow, and you see there are a lot of voices to blame here. The thing about pipes in general, though, is that once you get over your fear of them, you'll find they can work a certain magic on you.

They certainly kept up spirits in the new land, and also kept undesirable neighbors in their place. Never did these ideas take on more significance than when Canada sent several dozen pipe bands overseas during the First World War, which looked like droning on for some years. Just as in ancient times, the idea was to rally troops, and strike terror into the heart of the enemy.

One James Richardson, a Canadian piper of the 16th Battalion and ultimate Victoria Cross recipient, sprang to action when his company was approaching a Somme position. In full view of the enemy, he marched around and blared out *Reel of Tulloch*, all of which allowed his troop to cut through wire and capture their position. Any ancient Celtic army leader would have stood him a round for that.

Many, many times pipes blared away at the heads of regiments, and then pipers began forming bands, though found the old way of doing things had to give way to something more standardized and competitive. And that brings us to today's pipe bands, a particularly frightening phenomenon, especially when they're massed with drums, which can be found from Scotland to Canada, Argentina to China.

Bagpipes are not the only aerophones blown, squeezed and otherwise aerated in Celtic music. The Spanish-Celtic pig-castrator's panpipes deserve a mention but no description. Let's just go on to that whole other family of instruments that evolved from some primitive proto-Celt playing around with a reed, stick or bone he'd nicked, to blow along with those in China and Babylonia about 5,000 years ago.

Still, this might have remained an obscure thing, except that around 1907 in Berwick, Scotland, the media went mad over an excavated ancient brass whistle with six fingerholes, and companies like Clarke beefed up the modern tin-whistle industry.

These little instruments look laughably simple, but they have all sorts of techniques called crotcheting, quavering and tongueing you have to master if you want to sound anything other than shrill and ill. The tin whistle often is called the thin weasel, and one good thing about it is that it's small enough to easily lose. For a fuller, richer existence, there's the "low whistle," which continues to rise in popularity.

The flute has a high history as a 50,000-year-old holey femur fragment that continued to exist in some form or other, until 19th-century Bavarian musician Theodore Boehm started thinking "orchestral," and adding keys and things. But though you will see some fancier keyed flutes played by Celts, these players often tie down those keys and plug up those holes with currants, and many just chuck up the whole thing for a neo-old flute in a nice warm wood.

But the difference here also is what you do with it. Your typical classical flautist uses so little breath you wonder if he's even alive, while a Celtic flute player passionately embraces it, beefing up and accentuating his breathing, and snuffling all over the thing. It all ties in with Celtic sneeze-and-spittle words like *fleadh* and *feisanna,* events where people get together to blow all sorts of things. Some of them also blow the harmonica, which hails from southeast Asia around 3000 BCE, settled down in America, then sailed over to Ireland and its cousins.

As for the 18th-century German clarinet, with a nickname like "cabbage-stalk" it just had to filter out of military and classical applications right into the hands of folkies, primarily the Bretons. It often gets teamed with the bombarde, a fore-runner of the oboe. Occasionally things get mixed up and what you end up with is the bombard, an early cannon used to throw stone balls up to 500 lbs. in weight. This is a useful thing to have for bombardes that go on too long. Then you just pick up another clarinet and do a nice reedy *Kan ha Diskan* or *Sonneurs de Couple*.

In the mid 1800s, Belgian clarinetist Adolphe Sax started tinkering with his clarinets and fitting them out with oboe keys. He ended up with something that took France by storm, and America like a tornado – the saxophone. Now, it's plenty evident in jazz music, sometimes rock, but in Celtic music? Just take in the *Riverdance* orchestra, where those wailing alto and soprano versions show there can be a great deal of sax appeal to Celtic music.

But the sex appeal winner, believe it or not, is the accordion, which sometimes was called the "devil's box," and almost got itself X-rated. This was in Brittany, and it seems to have been because all their 19th-century dances, like polkas, waltzes and mazurkas, required chest-to-chest and belly-to-belly contact, as well as the liveliness of the right instrument. It was so right it actually muscled out the bagpipes here during the Great War, and many people did a real song and dance about that.

Accordion cousins the melodeon and concertina also got squeezed aplenty, the melodeon actually upstaging the bagpipes in the late 1800s. Breton and other European immigrants brought it to North America, and after they had made good, sent over a newer version to the folks at home. The melodeon also was one of few instruments girls could play without being considered forward. The whole thing became so big in Celtic circles that German manufacturer Hohner came forward to issue a model stamped with a big *Ceili* label.

The increasing use of the Australian didgeridoo in Celtic bands bodes ill that someone may do the same to it. The didgeridoo, traditionally hollowed by termites, is thought to be about 20,000 years old, or existing in Nature before man. It usually has a mouthpiece of beeswax, and you vibrate your lips against it to create a buzzing sound. It's so big it's difficult to lose by default or design, and it also makes the carnyx sound positively lyrical.

This ancient animal-headed trumpet, which rose from the blower's mouth like a banshee periscope, has been resurrected by Scottish musician John Kenny, and brought even into the world of contemporary jazz. Kenny's instrument of choice actually was the trombone, but he apparently saw a kinship here. As for Celtic music itself, though, it seems that almost anything that blows, goes.

\*

# Chapter 7

# MultiCeltural Instruments: Strung Out, Percussed and Perverted

## 1001 STRINGS

What's the difference between a violin and a fiddle? One's classical, one's folk, they're played differently, and the difference also comes down to whether or not there's foot-stomping, impromptu yells and whoops along with it.

Most whoop-it-up commoners may not know the instrument goes back to the ancient Egyptian or Greek *kithara,* and the Asiatic *ravanastrom* that in medieval Persia or Arabia got known as the *rebec,* which then went into rehab, another version. As time went on, there were European folk instruments called the *fithele, fiedel, vedel* or the *fitula,* which seemed to have little to do with what we think of as the violin.

It was the 15th-century *lira de braccio* that nudged things along toward what would become, by 1620 or so, the "violin" in Italy. At some point, it was brought by tourists and traders to Ireland, where it married an existing native *fidel,* and it had to happen because believe it or not the words violin and fiddle are etymologically related.

In Ireland, especially, it became a quavering, crotchety thing, which refers to the techniques like quavers and crotchets players dote on so much. Styles also can incriminate regions. County Donegal goes for staccato Highland stuff, a fallout of constant travel to Scotland;

Co. Sligo (whence a lot of musicians went to America) is bouncy and full of hope, Co. Kerry relaxed, East Galway downright wistful, and any of them cantankerous at times.

Scotland has similar variations, as well as those peculiar rhythms like Strathspeys and Scotch snaps. Celts often snap without their daily libations anyway, and this all goes back to laments for whiskey. Still, the Scots were able to put aside this obsession long enough in the 18th century to get strung out in a certain hybrid of popular dance and chamber-concert music.

Today there are fiddles galore, plain-and-simple or electrified to the nth non-fret, and you'll certainly hear them in *Riverdance* and *Lord of the Dance. Riverdance* also brought in the traditional Bulgarian fiddle, the *gadulka,* for its Eastern European and Russian segments. This one is so egotistical it won't be played on the shoulder, but stands on the lap to take a bow.

The harp seems to have existed in all places inhabited by men or spirits. Like the bagpipes, it debuted in ancient Sumeria, strung a lot of people along in Biblical times, touched down in just about every country in one form or another, and still plunks and ripples its way around the world. Still, it's especially associated with Celtic lands, and the Irish have made the stubby little folk version into a national symbol, as well as slapped it on Guinness beer bottles, their other national symbol.

Actually, the ancient Celts had a precursor to all this, and that was the lyre. It had two curved arms connected with a crossbar at the top. They weren't satisfied with that, as it was too Greek, and came up with something manlier. A status symbol for great lords, the harp also was prized by bards and minstrels. It was used at battles until someone realized bagpipes were much more effective.

Harps also had a lot to do with love, as they made great lays, and with magic. Many harps played themselves, even when there was a good bard around to do it. Those made from the breastbones of corpses often ribbed players and audience alike. Other harps leapt off the wall to kill people, and none of this seems to have dissuaded musicians through the ages.

Music-makers throughout the early middle ages also got quite obsessive about turning a simple harp into a thing of booty and embellishment forever. They carved, gilded (which goes back to about 4000 BCE), and embossed galore on various meaningful woods. Endless twisty designs with pop-eyed Danus, dragons, birds and fish – especially the Salmon of Knowledge – began to decorate harps' frames, and it's the kind of convoluted stuff you'll find also in illuminated manuscripts and Irish dance wear.

The Irish were proud enough to send their harps overseas, and Italian music historian Vincentio Galilei marvelled that this "most ancient instrument" was "excellently made," and in great numbers by great players. As Vincentio was the father of astronomer Galileo, it's obvious Dad had an eye for stars.

The *clarsach* was a metal-strung harp that plunked away even more in Scotland. "Teache him to harpe with his nayles scharpe" was the motto of the lay here. And as long fingernails against metal strings was the preferred method, you can guess what the ultimate punishment was. Medieval harps were modal and could not play accidentals – extra sharp, flat and natural notes outside the scheme of things – but when unlucky harpers got nailed and denailed, they played all sorts of things accidentally. So the harp came with some hassles. But even today, some musicians get all wired up in trying to master brass and bronze strings, over what they consider the gutless nylon version.

As time went on, the Irish harp got bigger and bigger. The Welsh, who sometimes felt inferior about their size, didn't like this, and came up with something called the triple harp, with three rows of strings, two parallels sounding the same note, with a row of accidentals between them.

There was plenty of intentional harping on themes in Celtic lands like Brittany, but apart from the Breton harpers that 12th-century English King Richard the Lionheart brought in for his coronation, no one else knew much about it until the early 1970s, when Breton musician Alan Stivell put out his *Renaissance de la Harpe Celtique* album, and electrified the concept.

Around this time, the bouzouki, from the *rebetiko* underworld musical art form of early 20th-century Greece, began showing up in Celtic folk-rock bands, though altered to the point no Greek would have anything to do with it. The bouzouki has a cousin called the cittern, and they're both loud, but for impact, nothing can beat the banjo. It travelled to the New World with African slaves, rang out on plantations, in blackface minstrel shows and early country music, then made a return trip across the ocean, to Ireland especially.

There's a similar American aspect to the mandolin. Hailing from Mesopotamia around 2000 BCE, it got influenced by the eastern wanderings of European medieval crusaders, then took on a new identity as the Italian mandorla. The great Stradivari even took time out from making violins to do a crack "mandolino" or two. But in the New World, it had a real heyday with the immigrants who brought it, a new middle-class hankering for exotic parlor instruments, and country music.

The lute, cello and viola da gamba also show up in Celtic music, and sometimes it was for statelier parlor stuff presented in the 18th and 19th centuries. But the cello, in early Scottish dance bands, also was considered a kind of accented drone, while ancient treatises regard the viola da gamba almost as a human voice, and *that* always has been a part of Celtic music.

Musical hybrids like the banjolin and mandocello also are evident in Celtic music, and there's no telling where this will end, so let's just forget them and give a few lines to the matter of the guitar. Though in some form and theory it goes back to the ancient Greek *kithara,* by all chord counts it seems to be a depressingly modern instrument for traditional Celtic music.

Many musicians dispute the matter, and they build a good case, with various "Celtic fingerpicking techniques," even reproducing droning and bagpipe ornamentation on their guitars, and, at least, getting the thing into a nice "dagdad" open tuning. As this arguably comes from the ancient Irish god warrior-god Dagda, the case gets even stronger. And in fact there's an entire music-book industry around the "Celtic guitar." So, let it stay.

## BEAT IT

One day someone banged a stick on a stone, a bone on a log. The drum was born. It got even bigger in the Celtic world when someone stretched a skin over a barrel to thump out *Mead, Myself and I.* The Celts kept the barrels, but wanted something more travel-friendly to beat it. It was banging on a farm sieve to loosen up the last fragments of wheat and chaff that did it, and that would change Celtic music history forever. This became the *bodhran.*

Some consider the bodhran – "bow-rawn" – a tambourine that lost its jingles, but this bourine-bodhran theory is not believed by those who say bodhran means "from deep within" or "deaf." Others suggest some swineherd was beating away on it one day, and his boar ran away. But don't let all this rusticity lull you into thinking this is a simple instrument to play. In fact, it's been suggested by some Irish music mavens that you learn another instrument or two first to get anywhere near proficient on this thumper.

The Cornish Celts have their own bodhran variation they call the *Kroeder Kroghan* or Crowdy Crawn drum. Like the bodhran, it seems to have started life as a kitchen or work tool, till someone realized the thing could be used to beat out a rhythm at happy hour after. And considering it's really part of a whole family of frame drums from China to Lapland, Mongolia to the Middle East, it would seem to be equally open to seasoning.

If you want to see any variety of drums in one place, look to *Riverdance.* The offerings vary from bodhran, to sets of two-and-four big boomy drums strapped around the neck, to a full crashing drum set-and-cymbals enough to make any big rock group gnash its collective teeth.

But in your atypical Celtic band too, you're also likely to find more exotic percussion, drums like the Moroccan *bendir,* the Nepalese *madal,* the Egyptian *riq,* the Indian *tabla,* and various finger-clickers and wood and bone clappers, scholastically known as concussion idiophones. Other percussing is done with real sole, and that's foot percussion, which has tapped right out of the *Riverdance* arena to become a star accompaniment on many strictly audio recordings.

Then there's the kind of percussion Jim Fidler, an innovative multi-instrumentalist from Newfoundland, Canada, did, for *Na Keen Affair,* an LP by renowned Irish musician Paddy Keenan. Fidler wanted something a little more, well, fluid-sounding, so with wires and mikes all around him, filled a bathtub with water, got down on his knees, and started beatin' it. This would seem to be all in keeping with a liquidated culture that rose out of the Danube and spawned things like *Riverdance.*

## AND IN A CLASS OF THEIR OWN

If you've ever hurd this instrument on a Celtic recording, you may have thought you were hearing some kind of bagpipe. The hurdy-gurdy does belong to the drone family. But it's got a clunky body, a piano key-board and a resined wheel that acts as a bow, as if its maker just didn't know when to stop. Anyway, you turn the wheel with the right hand and tinkle away on the ivories, while two strings produce a low keynote like the bagpipe.

Most likely of 13th-century Old French origin and known as the *vielle a roué,* it was called the "German lyre" by other countries, but the Germans said "No thanks" and shoved it back at the French. It was especial-ly popular in the 18th century at Marie Antoinette's court at Versailles, where they liked to play at being rustic. Classical composers played around with it, and it even was used in opera for local color. But these highfalutin examples aside, the Celtic folk arena is where it really drones on, and all without a monkey on its back (that version is a total corruption).

The hurdy-gurdy has a Swedish cousin, the *nyckel-harpa,* whose strings are bowed by the hand instead of a wheel, and which is called the sitar of the north, a nice Indo-European reminder. Its Norwegian neighbour the Hardanger fiddle is something that wants to be a violin (with four melody strings), but also a bagpipe, with four drones running through the instrument's body that vibrate in sympathy with the melody or bowed strings.

Many people have no sympathy at all for anything that drones, but both these instruments are creeping into Celtic music, and after all, the Keltoi did hit Scan-dinavia on their worldwide warpath.

The Celts may or may not have liked the hammered dulcimer, which has an Arabian-Chinese legacy of a few thousand years and is an ancestor of the piano (not allow-ed in traditional music). It helps if you're hammered to play anywhere from 30 to 50 strings on one big piece of board, and emerge from the dulcimer tuning process in one piece, but it has an unforgettable sound, so those who persevere for about 20 years are well rewarded.

But neo-Celts, take heart. There is a dulcimer for dummies, and it comes from American states like Kentucky and Virginia. When 18th- and 19th-century immigrant Scots, Irish, Germans and Swedes got over their seasickness, they remembered all sorts of homeland instruments, and one day someone put it all together into a new instrument, with three or four strings. It was called the mountain or Appalachian dulcimer, as well as the duckslammer, the hog-fiddle and worse. It's part of the human condition to make fun of what you love.

Traditionally played, the mountain dulcimer has a drone every bit as plaintive as the constant note in bagpipes. And now it's gone droning back over the water to the Scottish, Irish and all-over-Europe folky set, another example of how Celtic music is a full-circle thing.

It also happens to be an unbeatable all-in-one musicmaker. Besides those bagpipe pretensions, it's got modal scales, can sound like a harp, ring out like a banjo, and can, with endless effort and resin, be bowed like a fiddle. For the musician wannabe who just can't decide on an instrument after getting through Chapters 6 and 7, this is the one.

*

## Chapter 8

## Craic in the Community

At any time of the year, the ancient Celts were happy to get together for music, food, fun and drink, though there were certain times of the year when it was a really big thing. Those were the four big seasonal holidays, especially big in Ireland and Scotland.

*Imbolc* (which morphed into Candlemas and Ground-hog Day) in early February was when you endured purification rituals and sang up St. Brigid-the-multi-persona. For *Beltane* (May 1st) you extinguished all fires the night before, then made a needfire from the wood of nine different trees. After jumping through the blaze, everyone took embers from the fire to light their own hearths. Next morning, everyone danced around to bring up the sun.

*Lughnasa*, named after the sun-and-learning god Lugh (there couldn't be enough sun deities in a Celtic culture whose lands usually had heavy weather), heralded harvest time, and there was lots of dancing and feasting after their version of the Olympic Games. It also was the time of year when the "hiring fairs" let people find and give work, and get really heated up complaining about it. To let off steam, you could always reel around the sun to the tune of *Skip to my Lugh*.

*Samhain*, which would become Halloween, is when people got together to kill off excess livestock, went dancing between this world and the next, and made merry with songs like *Numbers of the Beasts*. Winter in general was a time to keep up spirits with impromptu costume-and-mask parties, an inevitable part of a shape-shifting culture.

One of the first singing-dancing get-togethers of Celtic history took place around 1000 BCE in Ireland, when someone called Ollam Fodhia, or "I Am Fuddled," was King. The event took place at the royal hall Tara, and was called *Feis Teamhair*, which means House of Music. It also was the beginning of words like *feis* and *fleadh*, musical words which you'll hear aplenty in damp climates, and of house parties in general.

But once they'd stopped sneezing, the organizers thought that, nice as it was to make merry, maybe they could bring a competitive aspect into it. To get the cont-testants, you had to offer prizes, and the most popular were a harp, a cow, a pig, and the lifting of a curse. It was the beginning of trying to outsing and outshine each other, and overall remained a friendly thing.

Just about the biggest kind of Celtic-music compet-itive get-together comes from one of the smallest Celtic lands, which is Wales. The *Eisteddfod* (which means more or less "gathering") started off as a kind of tournament of words in which aspiring and conspiring bards compet-ed against each other for the honour of inhouse exalta-tion. That is to say, employment, patronage, whatever you call it.

The first big one, which would supply many house-holds, was held by Welsh castle owner Lord Rhys ap Gruffydd in 1176, and he advertised for it about a year in advance. There were two chief contests here. One was poetic with a vengeance, to test the bards' skill in traditional and tedious Welsh meters; the other was loosely musical, open to minstrels and pipers of any nation. The grand prize was a chair which, it has to be said, was not much use to travelling musicians, but you might also get some nifty tokens from the castle's wardrobe and vintage departments.

In 1450 another big Eisteddfod was held at Carmarthen, and one Dafydd ap Edmwnd, a learned bard of North Wales, codified the rules, like why you must use as few vowels and as many doubled consonants as possible. At the really big events, held by Royal commission, all claimants to bardic privileges were thoroughly examined at the door, to be licensed or not. Those who didn't make the grade were classified as itinerants, who could seek their rewards door-to-door.

The Society of Bards behind it all had some pretty tough exams, and all along it had its critics, who objected to such strict requirements for conforming to a contemporary "high art notion." "Just let it flow!" was the exasperated cry sometimes heard. Competitions need rules, though, and in the end most people decided they'd rather have rules with their traditional music than no tradition at all.

But this sort of thing doesn't happen forever, and after the 1560s, things had deteriorated, with rural bards usually ending up carousing at some tavern, where they let everything flow. Also, pretty well any kind of regional-cultural thing that looked like fostering nationalism began to get royally stamped on. It sounded like the death knell for this musical happening.

And then, by the late 1700s, thanks to some Welsh nostalgia in London, the ancient customs were disinterred, and the whole bardic Eisteddfod thing got going again. It's mostly an annual event, and people come from all over the world. There still are critics, like those who claim the term Eisteddfod has come to mean mere colorful festivals, but it's a losing battle to try to stop people inappropriately using brand names.

However, no one else seems to have purloined certain regional Celtic specialties, like Cornwall's Hobby Horse song-and-celeb, which is all about fertility, and where trees like the maple, ash and sycamore reign supreme, not least in the star attraction, a big stick with a stallion's head. It's hardly a wooden affair though, as the whole thing is jangled up with accordions, melodeons and Crowdy Crawn drums, and "Crowdy Crawn," in fact, has just come to mean "a whole lot of fun."

Another Cornish oddity is the Helston Flurry (Floral), a noisy affair that blossoms and erupts on May Day to wind in and out of houses and outhouses and here, it seems, there's some parallel with Galicia's come-what-May *maios* structures found plastered with flowers all over town.

In every Celtic land there was dancing and music-making in homes, at crossroads, down by the rivers, to bring up the sun, and up in the stars, due either to drink or playful deities. Things could get a little wild even in structured events, too. In an 1899 Irish competition, blind piper Mickey O'Sullivan kicked up a fuss about tying with another contestant. He should have won, he insisted, but for the "fairy butter" he had eaten at his landlady Mrs. Moore's digs, and for the haunting influence of a "dead man's breeches." He got into quite a state about it, and that the judges took his case at all seriously indicates what a hold magic still had on the population.

In Scotland, there were plenty of piping competitions, often combined with cattle buy-and-sells called trysts, and by the 1890s, Scots also came up with something called The Mod, a competitive festival that's a lot more fun than the word's definition of "court or assembly."

In a less formal sense, there's the *ceilidh* or *ceili*. One is Scottish, the other's Irish, and just try to tell them apart when things get going. Both are loud and social, and if you've ever been at one you'll consider the word's etymological roots that mean "visit" and "companion" inadequate to describe it all. It's usually musical, though a lot of good talking in those singsong Gaelic voices also qualifies, and if it's really good you'll say the crack was exceptional that night. Those who stutter over hard C's can get by with describing it as *ri-ra*, another variation on communal good-feelings, while a similar gathering called *twmpath* often is the route to Welsh merriment.

The *seisiun* or session is a loosely-Irish thing that seems to have taken many Celtic lands, including North America, by storm, and something many feel is best done in pubs. Musicians sitting around shift closer together, there's the snap of instrument cases being opened and the crackle and pop of their contents being tuned up. Here a fiddle, there a bodhran, everywhere a flute or whistle...one starts, another joins in, and the thumping feet, bright eyes and twitching fingers all come together in a way to infect anyone within contagious range.

A whole body of music rolls out, one tune blending into another, everything going round and round like that convoluted embroidery. It's that circular Celtic music at work again, and good luck trying to extricate yourself when things really get going.

There's some debate of how old the session actually is. Some claim most music-playing in Celtic history was done solo, because how else could you show off all your own peculiar little ornamentations and designs? Those who claim the Celts did it all together drag up examples like early Eisteddfods and long-running bardic circles. At the latter, participants also traded otherworldly-music stories and occasionally played stuff right here on earth.

Both camps would probably agree, though, that musicians have played together for dances, which always needed that sort of thing. And when musicians began leaving home they especially realized there was both strength and fun in numbers. It happened a lot in 19th-century immigrant America, where you were glad to meet up with your own kind, and bang, blow and strum together.

To the outsider, a session seems a spontaneous thing, but it can be bound by as many rules and regulations as any *feisanna* or court in session. Humans being humans, too, sometimes what's also needed is a *feara-'ti*, basically someone in charge to ensure musicians, especially those with wind instruments, don't come to blows. In fact, the so-called humble session has so many ins and outs it's even come under the pens of ethnomusicology students who do entire theses on it, and ethnomusicologists who write entire books on it.

But those intimidated by all the etiquette, as well as by the sheer speed and expertise of many players, can take heart. If you look and listen, you can find slow sessions and jams all over the world, sometimes off the Internet, sometimes by just tracking down those in the know or *nos*. Any level of the musically inclined could easily session, slow-session, jam and bardic-circle their strings and guts out around the world. Typically it's the Irish and Scottish music that will hold it all together, though Wails, Brittany and other moaners are allowed.

If you actually go to Brittany, you'll find a culture that's tried to make up for the gradual disappearance of its folk clubs by organizing things like the *fest-noz,* where plenty of ZZZ songs are sung and droned. It began as a community village affair to look forward to after the day's chores were done, and it evolved by the 1950s as a more intensive way to keep the culture alive.

*Fest-noz,* for "feast-night," is your Breton version of a *ceili,* where the idea is to get drunk, get full on party food like cheese, pork and prune puddings, then dance all night to work it off. The whole thing has become modernized, and some of the traditionalists don't appreciate the way it's grown. Outside influences, they feel, dilute the pure Breton stuff, but it really wasn't doing too well on its own, so just put down their complaints to indigestion.

*Dastum* is a culture-collection association that puts on all manner of Breton lively events and the Breton "pardon" music-and-miracles kind of celebration has continued to pull in secular and sacred folk alike. Occasionally it gets secular to the point of being more a rock-band kind of thing, but many people seem to need this approach to keep tradition alive and ill.

Closely allied with its Breton cousin, the English region of Cornwall has been making noise for years with *troyls* — traditional Cornish music festivals that really grew when the trolls decided they'd try a human factor.

Back in Ireland, you'll find the outgrowth of what a determined post-WWII group called *Comhaltas Ceoltoiri Eireann* got going, certain song and dance festivals. After a *nos* eruption or two, they were named *Fleadh Cheoil,* which means feast of music, or close enough. *Fleadh* were centred around specific towns, with competitive scenarios to try to preserve the dying culture.

People had doubts about the first one. "Sounds like a fair without cattle," sniffed one detractor, but when these things got going, people came from all over, and village stock markets took a sharp rise. It's a huge concern today, with as many as 10,000 taking part and many times that coming to hear. But there's a long-standing *fleadh* tradition that the best music of all will be found in some little off-shoot village about a week after the main event. Sometimes, the improv and spontaneous just do it better.

But for thoroughly choreographed, you couldn't do better than the kind of maxed-out event of France's annual *Nuit Celtique* (Celtic Night). It's not something you're likely to forget soon, because it may include: the sound waves of a waggle-tongued carnyx, Scottish Highland and Breton pipe bands and superstars, electrified harps and wailing gaitas, roaring balladeers, screaming Galician *pandeireteras* with tambourines, and Welsh *cormeibion* choirs, Irish dancers and other European folk stompers, as well as full orchestra, trad band and drums of all degrees, while thousands roar their approval and madly wave regional flags beneath a galaxy of strobe lighting.

But even if you don't make it to the *Nuit,* you probably could find a Celtic show or festival somewhere around the world just about any day of the year. Though a lot of people in Ireland and Scotland have come to hate that C word as a catchall for anything folky, mournful and or synthesized, there's simply no other term that describes things so well. North Americans and almost anyone else around the world just adore the term "Celtic," and have plastered their continents with enough C-going associations and events to make you think they invented the word.

When people do tunes at get-togethers in Cape Breton, they discuss the songs' 18th- and 19th-century composers like neighbors just up the road. Cape Breton also is about the only place in North America where the G-word, Gaelic, lives on as a living language and culture, centuries away from the old homeland. However, Cape Breton's annual Celtic Colours Festival, which runs from square dances in community halls to grand stage concerts, welcomes the P, Q, Z and many other languages as well.

Wherever you go in Celtdom, you'll find groups of people playing music to link with the past and hope for the future. Perhaps The League of Celtic Galicia says it best. Their motto is "A people who forget their origins lose their identity; a people who lose their identity become dust," and *that* thought in a traditionally oral culture is scary enough to keep things going.

*

# Chapter 9

# Palaces, Patronage and Politics

Getting together to make music is one thing. A higher ideal running through the centuries was the idea to be nobly recognized.

That wasn't difficult for ancient chieftain Finn Mc-Cool and his army of balladeers, because they lived under the rule of Cormac Mac Airt, an Irish version of King Solomon who loved music so much he became a musician himself. Cormac was no egotist, though. He welcomed a chorus, whether it had bagpipes or not.

In the 10th-century Welsh court of Hywel Dda, the *penkerd* or chief singer, and inhouse harper, who both had come through with flying colors at a competitive *Eisteddfod,* were so exalted by their royal employer they often were mistaken for him, in one or other of his modes. Things were good in Scotland for Middle Aged musicians too. All Highland lairds had, besides a chatelaine and mastiff, 2.5 harpers and a bard who were allowed to have as much Scotch as anyone at the high table.

If you were hoping for inhouse musical employment in the Isle of Man, like harping or paying court to countesses, you had to be awfully sure of just what nationality was on the throne. This was before Man came into its own, and last year it might be Norse, this year Scottish, next Wednesday Welsh. Thus, you might dance up your song with a *ruidhle,* a Highland fling, or something with as few vowels as possible.

But this kind of political awareness was not really necessary in Galician-flavoured courts of Spain, at least, in the 13th-century time of King Alfonso X ("The Learned and Leaned-On"). Any national inclination was welcome, and Alphonso also filled his marbled halls with a congenial blend of Jewish, Muslim and Christian religions. The resulting musical mishmash gave him a truly Continental reputation.

Alfonso was especially strong on Marian miracles, and he composed and collected a big manuscript of Galician-Portuguese songs on the subject. If you could pull off some of this stuff, you really had it made. But while he was working away on it — and it took some time — he was happy to have strung-out people of every persuasion harping on various themes, banging on bombos and tamborils, and blowing their brains out with various woodwinds and bagpipes.

His namesake Alfonso III of Portugal, welcomed musical stuff like *cantigas de amor,* and *cantigas de amigo* for those who thought platonically. He had a fondness for Breton lays and Arthurian tales, so Celts who could produce these sentiment and derring-do pieces were welcome. Galicians were especially welcome, as they could get close to understanding Portuguese, but the court aspired in its own way, to be as diverse as the scene in bigger Spain.

Alfonso III's son Dinis was renowned himself in the Iberian Peninsula as a crack poet, and he welcomed anyone else good enough with words and music to ultimately join him in the famous *cancioneiros,* or song books.

All in all, bards and harpers were well-respected for their ballads and lays in the Celtic world for some time. Annals and records in Ireland and Scotland from the late 1400s also, if you can decipher the writing, show they were well-paid. Even those who didn't make it as honored inhousers generally got a good reception. It all was considered high-art music, not written as such, be-cause not many people wrote in those days, but really put up on a pedestal rather than folked around with.

Pipers got a mixed reaction. They were noisy, com-pared to harpers, and that might be good or bad. There were some warning notes to heed, when 14th-century Royalty began carving out statues to forbid pipers to en-ter The Pale, the English dominions in Ireland, and making anyone found giving shelter to them guilty of a major offence.

But even if England's Henry IV passed a weighty statute in good Norman French denouncing piping and minstrelsy "vagabonds" in Wales, his successor Henry V-of-Agincourt fame liked pipes, travelled with them, and apparently used them to play stirring national music on the night before this famous battle fought on French grounds.

Scotland's King Alexander and David II employed pipers, and the country's succession of Jameses had mixed reactions to music. James I, who did his thing from 1424-37, not only liked the pipes, but played them himself. At one point he also hired a Welsh harpist, one Robert ap Huw the Paranoid, who wrote a lone manu-script in his own code of indecipherable symbols. It was a serious detraction to preserving this kind of music for posterity (though it's provided endless fun for music his-torians through the ages since then, to try to interpret). As ap Huw apparently composed it in the presence of James, then refused to explain it, there's some evidence that James asked for his money back.

His son James II (1437-60) really reigned on every-one's parade by passing an act for the suppression of minstrels, but things got better with James III, who actually knighted his musical favourites. This did irritate his nobles, who demanded the King give up these music-makers or not count on aid in an invasion by the English.

James called their bluff, and the nobles broke in and hanged the lot over a nearby bridge. This son-of-a-royal had learned the hard way there was a right and wrong way to court musicians.

James IV was more careful about the whole thing, but he did perish at the Battle of Flodden against the English in 1513, so it didn't do him much good. However, he'd been so fond of minstrels they in turn would create a famous piping lament, *Flowers of the Forest*, to commemorate his destruction.

James V, who succeeded Dad at the ripe age of one year old, not only liked pipes but played them, though his scribe, Master Bellenden, grumbled that "synging, fydlyng and pypyng" made men "soft" and were inappropriate for those of "hye estate." James VI (also James I of England, which is where it starts to get muddy), thought so too, and tried to break up the whole bardic thing, along with the drinking that inevitably accompanied it.

England's Queen Elizabeth I (1533-1603) also put her royal foot down. Even though Bess would admit to liking a Gaelic jig in her own court, she felt duty-bound to stomp on the Irish and keep them from speaking their own tongue, marrying, owning land, trying to better their course in life, and from piping up and droning on. She kept her deputees busy outlawing Irish bards and musicians. Often, it was easiest just to hang them, rather than take the chance their music might foster Irish nationalism and dissent. A half-century or so later, Oliver Cromwell seconded the motion, and most brutally, too.

The Church also went after the music-makers. In Scotland in 1679, a group of women went to the stake because they supposedly had danced around to the bagpipe music of the Devil and "other witches" at a moonlight event. With this kind of press, it's not hard to see why the bagpipes often fell out of favor.

They also came to be considered seditious. This is what the English pulled out, to execute one Scottish "rebel," musician James Reid, just after the Battle of Culloden in 1746. The defence protested that he wasn't carrying any arms, but the Court said that because highland regiments never travelled without a piper, in the eyes of the Law the bagpipe was an instrument of war (which the Scots really always knew) and the piper must pay. Most other Scots stopped playing the pipes, at least in public, after Culloden. The conquering English army was led by one "Butcher" Duke of Cumberland, and it just made things too dicey.

Things improved by Queen Victoria's reign in the 19th century. After her beloved consort Albert died, Victoria developed a real thing for Scotland and a low-class fellow called John Brown. He played the pipes, and it's because of Victoria's fondness for Johnny's skirts and skirls that Highland bagpipes were introduced to the British Army, and that's where *that* started – those endless parades, those endless albums, those courtyard pipers who get the day going for royalty in residence.

Harpers generally got greater favor throughout history. Ruairi (Rory or Roger) Dall O'Cahan (1570-1650), who was born in County Derry, Ireland, preferred Scotland, especially the royal residence of Holyrood Palace, and he was so good that James VI, who usually banned bards, let him play. Rory Dall had it made, which was just as well, as "Dall" meant "blind," and there wasn't much else in those days you could do without eyes in the front of your head.

Rory took to composing "ports" for the nobility, while everyone drank port, and was quick to find a song for every occasion. One of his most famous pieces is a handsome tune called *Tabhair Dom do Lamh,* or *Give Me Your Hand.* It's a kiss-and-make-up song for one Lady Eglintoun, with whom he had fallen out over some insult or

81

other, and still is used in reconciliatory situations as well as poker scenarios.

Rory died in great state in some Scottish manor, leaving behind his harp and silver tuning key for posterity. Another blind harper named Echlin Kearne fumbled his way to the house to collect these items. He sold the harp in Edinburgh and drank away its profits, and it's a sad ending to the royal Rory story. Fortunately, Rory had already written a song called *O'Cahan's Lament,* which showed a similar mindset to those MacCrimmon pipers who went into battle armed with their own death songs, so his death was lyrical in that sense.

Another Rory Dall, Roderick Morrison (1656-1713), originally had dreamed of becoming a man of the cloth, but smallpox-cum-blindness inspired or resigned him to take up the harp, and he served the chief of the Mac-Leod clan in the Isle of Skye. He also had the vision to please the famous MacCrimmon family, who still considered the light stuff beneath them. This *piobaireachd*-piping clan really loved the harp, so we might as well assume the lot really were descended from a harper named Cremona.

The two Rorys have become, in many music-historians' minds, a composite of one semi-mythical figure. They're clearer about Welshman John Parry, who harped for English King George III, no less. Parry also was admired by classical composer Handel, inspired poet Thomas Gray to write *The Bard,* and ended up with one impressive CV. Parry laid on a lot of airs from all this, but applied himself enough to publish a book called *Antient British Music,* without any semi-composites, in 1742.

What happened to a lot of harpers, though, is about as sad as what happened to the pipers, even if not as many harpers were hanged for sedition. When Gaelic patrons lost their wealth to new English landowners after the 1600s, the bardic order collapsed, and the map became dotted with luckless lay-singers.

Many of them cried out for succor to their patron saint, sixth-century Herve of Brittany. But as Herve was still busy reinventing the Breton scene, even long after his death, answer came there none. A musical society that always had had one foot in the magic arena became even more disillusioned. Demeaning as it was, harpers had to learn to function on a freelance basis. John Parry did all right for himself, but he couldn't hold a tuning key for entrepreneurship to a certain 17th-18th century Irish colleague.

The first thing this one did was change his name from *Toirdhealbhach O' Cearbhallain* to the snappier Turlough O'Carolan. Along with a guide, a horse, and words of encouragement from a Mrs. McDermott Roe, who'd got him going on this career path (and who couldn't afford to hire him as an inhouse performer even if it was in vogue), he would set out over Ireland to make his fame, in what would be a 45-year career as a traveling Gaelsman.

Turlough was not the best harp player in the world, but a Squire Reynolds suggested he try his hand at composition. The first such, *Si Beag, Si Mhor,* referred to the fairies who fought on neighbouring hill mounds. Great for the Celtic books, but Turlough couldn't live on that.

He mapped out a plan and began to compose songs specially for his patrons, in the conviction that flattery was the sincerest form of flattery. These were called planxties — *Planxty George Brabazon, Planxty Fanny Power, Planxty Your Esteemed Lordship,* etc. As Cromwell had done his best to smash the old Gaelic order, Turlough's audience was more usually Anglo than Irish. Not all the English were intolerant, though. Many had a great appreciation for fine music, but you just had to play harp in their court. They had the money, even if it was the much-derided new money, and Turlough had himself, his guide, his horse and his harp to feed.

Evidently, he was well-fed enough to produce an impressive body of airs, laments, marches, mushy stuff galore, and at least one concerto. Influenced by the Continent, he periodically went for Baroque, and Italian masters Vivaldi, Corelli and Geminiani. It was just what people who wanted to be thought of as educated and aristocratic wanted to hear.

The music Turlough left the world would be responsible for a good chunk of the repertory of many Celtic musicians today. Renowned California harper Patrick Ball donned period garb to begin performing a one-man theater piece, *O'Carolan's Farewell to Music,* as told through the eyes of Turlough's crony Charles McCabe. For most modern audiences, it's really a hello to the music, and a splendid way to get introduced to it, too.

Scottish fulltime professional Highland-tradition storyteller Paraig MacNeil, who some time ago donned the historical belted-plaid-and-cloak kit, also has a foot in another era. He's acquired the title of first Honorary Bard/*Seanchaidh* to the Clan Gregor Society for centuries. This kind of role may have become diluted over the centuries, but it's still a nice link with the past.

And finally, Irish chief Red Hugh O'Donnell, who fled to Spain in 1601 after the Battle of Kinsale in Ireland, did feel he should at least honor the ongoing *espanol* assistance he'd had against the English. He immediately began lobbying for a Spanish dance segment to appear in the upcoming extravaganza *Riverdance.*

\*

# Chapter 10

# More Craic Composers, Composters and Blind Bards of Yore

A great chunk of modern-day Celtic musicians' repertoires comes from the previous chapter's court reporters and performers, but there were any number of other obsessed harpers, fiddlers and pipers doing their thing.

Early contenders for the books include the ninth-century Bardd Glas Geraint or "Geraint the Blue Bard," whose fame grew so much in the centuries after, that when Geoffrey Chaucer penned his 14th-century *House of Fame* potboiler, he placed Welshman Geraint right up in the minstrels' gallery, with other well-known harpies like Orpheus, Orion and Chiron. Geraint's fame continued to grow, in folk ballads that with a bit of tweaking, made it big in England and Scotland.

Nothing as big, though, as 15th-century Henry the Minstrel's masterpiece, an ode to Scottish brave heart Sir William Wallace that ran 11,681 lines and 12 volumes. Because Henry, or "Blind Harry" as he was called, wrote this epic 150 years after the war-leader's death, his research is suspect. Still, his work endeared him to Scottish Kings, and a few centuries later, to Hollywood royalty, which got actor Mel Gibson quite blue about the whole thing in *Braveheart*.

Harry was a member of Blind Bards Inc., which really got going with the invention of smallpox. Barding was about the only profession a blind person could practise, though if you were poxed in adulthood, you had some making-up to do to achieve standards usually set in toddlerhood. But you also got a leg up in a society that generally considered the blind to have special powers. Certainly the two Rory Dalls did all right for themselves, and that Irish patron-pleaser Turlough O'Carolan was master at working through a disability.

The blind harper phenomenon was a press-worthy part of the Belfast Harp Festival, first held in 1792. Its organizer, merchant James Dungan, had heard about yearly pipe festivals in Scotland and thought he could bring the idea home, with a more refined touch, to Ireland because as he lamented to a friend, "Poor Erin's harp is decreasing."

Promising good pay for contestants, it did haul in only ten contenders. Of them, aged 15 to 97, six were blind. The strongest holdout for doing things the old way, i.e., with long fingernails against metal strings, was *Donnchadh O Hamsaigh*, or Denis O'Hampsey, the oldest. Denis, blinded by the blight as a child, had harped for Scotland's Bonnie Prince Charlie though in the contest played only Irish music.

In fact, he was the only contestant whose repertory and style really came close to the old way of medieval harping. Denis really was born 500 years too late, and by the end of the competition was all strung out, with even less left for the girl he'd married in his 80s, who just wanted to string him along.

Still this new awareness awakened by the BHF made it a good time for other harpers, and if you're unlucky enough to get hold of the writings of harper Arthur O'Neill (1737-1816), you'll see why. O'Neill, who'd actually been blinded by a doctor's ministrations, somehow had the vision to put together some exhaustive memoirs praising and criticizing his peers.

Arthur represents the bookish end of things while others like Patrick Byrne (1797-1863), who got blindly going at 26, wanted the spotlights. Patrick bagged Royal performances and public concerts, sat for portraits and became an out-and-out ham playing an "ancient Celtic bard" in historical tableaux.

And Iain Dall MacKay (1656-1754) was so good at the famous MacCrimmon College of Piping in Skye, jealous pupils teamed up to throw him over a 30-foot cliff. By some miracle he escaped serious injury, and went on to be an excellent if somewhat bruised artist.

Cornish storyteller Anthony James took note of the whole thing, and later took a boy and dog to hit the Cornwall circuit, which had a lot of cliffs. As these were isolated parts, he was greeted with glee and quickly became a minor star. Anthony sang "drolls" about people and places outlandish even by Celtic standards, and drew small crowds with his old droll-teller's *crwth,* that is, "crowd" or fiddle.

Blindness somehow gave many performers the push they needed to succeed. Carl Hardebeck, the Big Blind Bard of Belfast, played the harmonium like an angel. Poet Antoine O Raifteiri fiddled and sang his songs in west-Ireland country houses, made a living at it, and was immortalized by poet Yeats in *The Tower.* Scotland's John Riddell was so good with the fiddle the upper classes called him a violinist.

There were a lot of famous fiddlers, and chief amongst them was the Gow clan. Niel Gow, who could see well enough to leave the family plaid-weaving business behind, began fiddling around age nine in 1730, at 18 won a fiddling contest, and really got going around 60. A real social animal, he seems also to have been the great equalizer. There always was a certain awkwardness at the country ball between nobles and humbles till Niel came out and began playing his stuff, from reels to jigs to strathspeys, often pulling in his brother Donald on cello.

After a historic meeting with poet Robert Burns, he created *Niel Gow's Farewell to Whiskey,* and as Robbie liked his drink too, it was a dual lament. Whiskey often was in short supply or banned, and this was a big concern, but Niel directed some pathos towards humans as well. He wrote *Niel Gow's Lament for the Death of his Second Wife, Niel Gow's Lamentation for James Moray of Abercairney,* (which goes by many similar titles), and overall did about 90 tunes, dabbling in magic with *Fairy Reel,* which was transformed into a dance. Niel is thought to have "borrowed"some of his tunes, but in spite of that had a big song, *Caledonia's Wail for Niel Gow,* done in his honour.

Niel's son Nathaniel, who often moonlighted as a band cellist and at 20 got the plum job of Herald Trumpeter, also did the social-circuit scene. He even became a favorite of that portly windbag the English Prince Regent-cum-George IV. In spite of patronage and gifts galore, Nathaniel tended to go bankrupt, but he certainly was solvent enough when it came to songwriting. He did about 200 tunes for all occasions, while *his* son Neil penned songs like *Bonnie Prince Charlie* and *Flora MacDonald's Lament.*

But it was James Scott Skinner, born in 1843, who gave the whole scene a real *Celtic Idol* quality. By the age of nine, J. Scott was a member of hot Manchester boys' band Dr. Mark's Little Men, but he also was a kilted punk who regularly got booted off musical tours for fighting. He managed to stop the fisticuffs long enough to write *Highland Polka,* which hit the hit parade when he was 17. It was followed by *The Ettrick Vale Quadrilles, A Guide To Fashionable Dancing, The Harp and Claymore* and almost 600 more. Somehow, he'd managed to tame his spirit long enough to contribute to posterity.

J. Scott went on to play for Queen Victoria at Buckingham Palace, and also went to America to fiddle around.

In the end, he returned to the Highlands, where he was never happier than when knee-deep in a salmon pond, composing ditties to the wisdom of fish. He did, though, remain obsessed by someone known as *The Bonnie Lass O' Bon Accord*. It was his best-known piece and ultimately music to die for, as its opening bars decorate his gravestone in Aberdeen.

But for publicity, as well as simultaneous seducing, composting, piping up and fiddling around, no one can beat Robert Burns.

Sometime after he was born in 1759, Robert chucked up the family ploughing biz, shortened his given name "Burnes" for better PR, learned just enough French to put on airs, and embarked on a series of mad love affairs. He was learning, in other words, to be a musician. Robbie loved and sang up lassies like Jean, Peggy, Clarinda, and Highland Mary, and cried out things like, *I Reign in Jeanie's Bosom!* which became a song. He also sailed off to a Jamaican plantation for good rum and more inspiration, though his bagpipes were not welcome there.

Burns burned the midnight oil composing many songs to drink, but also commented more seriously on *Such A Parcel of Rogues In A Nation*, *The Solemn League and Covenant*, and *The Poet's Reply to the Threat of a Censorius Critic*. When he was feeling particularly bedeviled, he wrote things like *Tam O'Shanter*, a witchy piece the Church came down hard on him for, especially when he played it with bagpipes. He didn't care, just went on to write or be associated with some 600 songs, the most famous of which is *Auld Lang Syne*, and which means "long ago."

It arguably is seconded by *A Man's A Man For a' That*. This was sung at the state opening of Scottish Parliament at its comeback in 1999 after a mere 300 years, and we can be sure Robert just tippled in his grave.

For lack of better PR, not everyone in music history fared so well. Seventeenth-century Irishman Thomas Connellan supposedly composed over 700 tunes, but we can scrape up only a few of them today. Thomas liked Scotland enough to tartan-up some Irish tunes, which is how *Limerick's Lamentation* became *Lochaber No More.* This renaming and reworking of songs would play a major part in Celtic song history, and it's got a lot of people quite muddled. However, Tom died unknowing the extent of this, and actually died in a castle. Unfortunately, he was buried in an unmarked grave, a kind of analogy for what can happen to so much traditional music, unless it's dug up, dusted off, and given new blood and whiskey.

Continental influences, as we saw with Turlough O'Carolan, also made for interesting music, though aff ected musicians themselves in different ways. David Murphy, an O'Carolan peer who called the blind harper's music "like bones without beef," was conceited enough playing in his own homeground of Leinster, but then he went over to France to play before King Louis XIV and soak up various *je ne sais quoises,* and from then on came back acting as if he was better than anyone else.

On the other hand, 19th-century John Thomas of Wales hit the Continential circuit to hang around with classic examples like Rossini, Liszt and Berlioz, but it didn't spoil him. In fact, he spent ten years putting together a collection called *Welsh Melodies for the Harp,* which was published in 1862. There's no place like home, Thomas thought, as he harped and scratched away.

A similar patriotism existed in Galicia, especially among blind fiddlers who didn't like to travel. Flocencio o Cego Dos Villares ("the blind of Dos Villares") and his fellow fiddlers were *picaro,* streetwise survivors who often teamed up with tambourine and hurdy-gurdy players at the fairs.

Flocencio and his cronies cranked out dance music, Romance ballads of love, lust, larceny, murder, and mockery, and also cut any number of political scenarios to ribbons with their satire. The public loved it, and late 20th-century musician Pancho Alvarez resurrected the whole thing, with an LP tribute to Flocencio.

Galicia also had a good 19th-century thing going with one Eduardo Pondal, who was adamant that the Gallegos, inhabitants of Galicia, were not the Spanish-Portuguese hybrids many people made them out to be, but definitely Celts. He wrote singable romantic epics to prove it. Eduardo would be proud to know his efforts would live on to become a profitable tourist trade featuring wild-kilted-Keltoi posters, and regional story-and-drama events called *Queimadas*. These are best done over a flaming bowl of liquor, which seems to heat up tradition like nothing else. A needfire, if you like.

## ADDENDUM: LADIES A LA MOAN

When the ancient Irish Queen Medb (Maeve) raised war against the province of Ulster, she sang such a howling song of horror that a hundred warriors dropped dead from fright before the fight began. In fact, some of history's best vocals have been done by women.

The banshees generally were female, and there were women-only bardic collectives with allowances made for female hormones. Any self-respecting Celtic funeral procession came with a knock-em-dead keener behind the cadaver.

Women also became known as such good carriers of storytelling and songs, that more than one male bard beefed he saw no need to chronicle a local battle because the girls had sung it up before the corpses turned cold. And in Galicia, *riveiranas* traditionally churned out such wild music with tambourines no male was gutsy enough to go anywhere near it.

Others, like 15th-century Welshwoman Gwerful Merchain, really drew the men. Gwerful kept a tavern, a and wrote some of the most explicit verses you ever heard. She meant it as thought-provoking poetry and hoped to publish in serious and uncensored volumes in case the hospitality business didn't work out, but never doubt that at happy hour her stuff got sung up and thrown up by the boys. Still, most of the memorable female songwriters here seem to be great Scots, with, unfortunately, some doom and gloom.

Mary MacLeod (1615-1707) of the Harris Isles, who did the requisite lamenting and poetry for Highland estates, was the descendent of a clan chief, and her most famous song a paean to a snuff-mill. You'd think all this would pave the way to endless respect, but she was just one of those people who don't seem to have the gift of pleasing. She was banished to the Isle of Mull, which she sang about long before Sir Paul McCartney did. When she died, she was buried face-down under a pile of stones, though the MacCrimmon family piped up with *Mary MacLeod's Lament,* when they had a little spare time between pupils.

For Lucy Johnston (1760-1797), the major struggle was in trying to avoid just being grist for other people's songs, as she was one comely lass. Robert Burns adored her, and she stole the floor at the famous Edinburgh Dance Assembly. But Lucy had a musical brain, too, and plenty of ambition. She was smart enough to write tunes like *Miss Lucy Johnston's Compliments to Niel Gow*, which got her right into that gentleman's book, and it was the start of being taken seriously. After that, she got called back time and again with both fiddle and feathered pen.

*Will Ye No' Come Back Again?* is a Scottish song as poignant as they come. The 18th-century Lady Caroline Nairne wrote it for His Highness Bonnie Prince Charlie, who had fled over the water to France after his army was wiped out in 1746. Caroline wasn't even born until 20 years after this, but she was fixated on the Prince, no doubt about it, and spent much of her life composing weepers like *Charlie Is My Darling*, and *Who'll Be King But Charlie?*, a song that would go on to pick up umpteen American verses as *Weevily Wheat*. That song is all about baking a cake for Charlie, and judging by the title, it wasn't a very good harvest year.

Mary MacPherson was an agriculturally inclined balladeer who came stomping out of Skye to champion various Celtic causes, like the crofters' struggle to get justice during the land-reform wars of the 1880s. The fact she got thrown in jail in Inverness for supposedly nicking her employer's personals, became just more grist for her song mill. Revisionist history claims she promptly composed *Cami-knicker Caoineadh,* and it was a bit of a poke at Mary, a big earthy woman who was hardly a pinup model.

The truth was, this song was a reworking of one applied to harper Rose Mooney, one of the few remaining itinerant female minstrels in the late 18th century, who performed at the Belfast Harp Festival. That chatty memoirist Arthur O'Neill comments that before one event she pledged "her harp, her petticoat and her cloak." But it seems the real culprit here was Rose's maid Mary, who took advantage of her employer's blindness by pawning any article she could get her hands on, for drink. All in all, not bad material for a *cami-lament.*

\*

# Chapter 11

## The Great Celtic Collection Agency

From Day One the Celts were collecting songs, sagas and ballads, and putting them in some sort of memory bank they could draw upon.

But there was just so much you could do in an oral culture or as a one-off monkish kind of thing. Song harvesting had the potential to become real industry only after the printing press was invented in 1450 CE, and there were plenty of people who wanted to preserve the past with it. Broadside ballads, or song sheets, fluttered around at fairs, but something more permanent was needed.

One of the first to go at the Celta-collecting whole hog was Allan Ramsay. Born in 1686 in Lanarkshire, Scotland, he was a wigmaker who ultimately became so enamored with collecting old ballads and songs people constantly begged him to "Keep your hair on, Al!" Wig askew, he became a bookseller, all the better to push his first volume *The Tea-Table Miscellany.* As he'd published these songs without airs, he followed up *Miscellany* with *Musick for Allan Ramsay's Collection of Scots Songs,* and the industry began to reel and roll off the presses.

In Ireland, things really got going with Edward Bunting, a superstar of collectors, if there's such a thing. Born in 1773, it was apparent when he was in bunting that he was something of a genius. By 11, he played a mean church organ, but even though he was classically trained, was fascinated with the medieval music of the old harpers.

The 1792 Belfast Harp Festival's organizers, who ached to preserve Ireland's best from the past and hope for the future, decided to take a chance with the 19-year-old Edward as scrivener/court transcriber for this momentous event. "Go to it," he was told, but also was cautioned to take down the airs and songs *as is,* and not even think about putting any on by adding a single note of his own to these old melodies.

Bunting did his best, though he had to write the Gaelic words phonetically, which made for much merriment amongst the Old Guard. Then he started going out into the backwoods and byways to collect more gems. He knew he'd found his real calling, and began publishing big works like *A General and Generous Collection of the Ancient Music of Ireland,* really the first extensive publication of traditional Irish music. Denis O'Hampsey, that hoary old harper, kindly hung on to the age of 110 to provide Bunting with some real keepers. One of them was *Aisling an Oghfir,* a melody that would enter the book of contenders for the origins of famous song *Danny Boy.*

Ed was a passionate collector, but he couldn't resist tinkering around with melodies on the theory that anything that sounded nice and old could be made to sound even nicer for the Sunday-afternoon parlor scenario. In the end, Bunting's medieval interests got snowed under by his theory that the easier to harmonize a piece was, the purer it must be.

It really means that a lot of very pure pieces got mucked about with. You might think a little harmony is a nice thing, but that was not the Celtic way of doing things. It was original melody all the way. Still, these tarted-up arrangements were considered more up to date, and a lot of the public liked all the pastry overlays.

George Petrie, a contemporary of Bunting, was another we can both laud and blame for what he did with Irish music. Like Bunting, he collected lots of it. He also was president of a club with the catchy name of The Society for the Preservation and Publication of the Melodies of Ireland, which published *The Ancient Music of Ireland* (1855).

But he was an outsider who didn't speak Irish, and also big on harmony. He played around with trad music for piano and let a "professor of music," the kind of person most traditionalists would gladly shoot on sight, "correct" it. Besides collecting and playing around with ancient airs, he was known for a long-running feud with Edward Bunting. Bunting refused to help out George as editor on George's collections because he didn't want to be associated with any project that was not strictly his baby.

In turn, Petrie began publicly knocking all Bunting's theories, then peevishly got another collector called Patrick Weston Joyce to contribute to his collections, but Patrick took off to do his own thing, with compilations like *Ancient Irish Music* and *Irish Peasant Songs in the English Language.*

One Joycean song that became very popular was *The Leprechaun,* and it would become big in America as a nostalgic longing for an Ireland that never really was, or at least hadn't been for some time. Patrick added pianoforte accompaniment, fiddled with the notation of songs, and in his spare time sat back to both pity and admire his colleague Patrick Lynch, who'd decided to start collecting music from bagpipers.

Collectors like Frances Tolmie and Keith MacDonald wandered through Scotland's Isle of Skye and got some good cloud-and-crowd songs, but were eclipsed by Marjorie Kennedy-Fraser. Marjorie was from a musical touring family, turned her daughter Patuffa into a harper, and learned Gaelic. Mother and daughter tramped around after field workers and into the Hebridean cottages looking for old folk songs. Marj even used an early cylindrical recording machine, and did her best to follow the lax rhythms of folk as they warbled out the songs they remembered.

Her four-volume effort *Songs of the Hebrides,* came out in 1909, 1917, 1921 and 1928, though another collector named Donald Ferguson tried to outdo her with *Songs from the Farthest Hebrides.* Marjorie was praised by poet W.B. Yeats and others for her efforts to be "true to the original." But she'd begun to look at her folksong findings as rough diamonds she could polish up and cut with a better rhythm and tempo to present in a concert hall.

Quite simply, the tunes as they were often didn't sound "right" to the ears of collectors, who tried to make modal melodies conform to chromatic standard major and minor scales. This business of adding harmonies for accompaniment on piano and pianoforte also sucked some of the character out of the songs.

One who seems to have escaped the critical axe is Maria Jane Williams (1795-1873) of Wales. She got herself patronized by bishops, dukes, earls and countesses, but seems not to have sold out. Song critic Lucy Broadwood stated that for the most part, the Druidical-and-other songs Jane collected were "in their wild and original state." This may be because Jane was something of a wild original herself. She was a real dish, and had a maidservant, Fanny Baker, who seems to have been her illegitimate daughter, by either an earl or a good-looking gardener. Maybe Jane was just too busy partying to hun ker down to harmonic embellishments, modal destruction and other horrors.

Gavin Greig (1856-1914), a relative of the classical composer Edvard (though by that time, the family was more Scottish than Norseish) did quite well himself. He spoke the local dialects of northeast Scotland, and was good at loosening up taciturn folk, and getting the songs down much as they were given. Other collectors like Rev. Baring Gould, and English composers Ralph Vaughan-Williams and Percy Grainger also are among those who didn't tinker with tradition in their assiduous collecting. But good or bad, the whole loose collective helped save a largely oral culture from fizzling out in the fens.

The one who stoked it the most outrageously is 18th-century James MacPherson, known as the resuscitator of the ancient Ossian ballads. He set out to make them as Scottish as possible, which many felt kilt the whole idea. More than a few people also suspected he'd forged the "ancient manuscripts" he worked from.

Still, when many a lay was done, MacPherson had in effect created a kind of Gaelic *Illiad*-and-*Odyssey* all in keeping with folk culture. His *Fragments of Ancient Poetry collected in the Highlands of Scotland translated from the Gaelic or Erse language* is still exciting debate amongst scholars, who have a grand time squabbling over whether he was true to the Ossian or the Asinine.

Brittany had its own versions of Ossianic-type legends, and these were rescued in the 19th century by nobleman Hersart de Villemarque and ultimately published in his impressive 1839 collection, *Barzaz Breizh.* Farmers, fishermen and the folk dishing up the dockside oyster-and-pancake breakfasts had been sowing and saucing the old music for centuries, and that's what Hersart wanted. It wasn't just a passing rich-and-idle whim, as he ended up devoting years to following ploughs and payellas all over the place, egged on by his mother, who'd started it all by telling him bedtime stories-and-*breizh* for years.

Hersart collected Galician, Arthurian and Antidiluvean legends and heroic ballads galore, happily tramping literary roads and rivers and pumping all sorts of folks. But in the end – and isn't this a familiar refrain? – there were many people who accused Hersart of, if not exactly making the whole thing up, at least tweaking the songs, or cleaning up the parts he found objectionable.

Certainly, he is known to have substituted nicer phrases for certain "vicious expressions," or at least of "less poetic" verses. In his defence, he claimed Scottish poet Sir Walter Scott had done exactly the same thing in his *Scottish Minstrelsy,* so why shouldn't he, Hersart, wield equal editorial rights? Actually, Hersart did a good job, and he also got his stuff into Brittany's premiere folkloric collection run by the *Dastum.*

He was followed by François-Marie Luzel (1821-95), a scholar of popular theatre who collected and published about 400 pieces from northern Brittany, and seems to have kept things more as he found them, but just never achieved the PR Hersart did. Other Bretons scooped and sorted old songs and poems, though World War I had a numbing effect on the collecting as well as on just about everything else, and things wouldn't pick up again until the 1950s-60s universal folk movement.

Many Galician collection agencies traditionally have doubled as folk choirs. It's handy to know what you want to find, and to be able to instantly sing it up once you've found it. Collector Casto Sampedro y Folgar collected at least 450 tunes in his *Cancionero Musical de Galicia,* and many of them were interesting enough to now have been jumped upon by a new wave of Gallego music industry go-getters.

One of the real biggies of Galician culture, the entire collection of Middle-Aged composer Martin Codax's *Cantigas de Amigo* (Friend's Ballads) in the so-called Vindel Parchment came out of 700-year-obscurity when it was discovered wrapping a copy of a book by philosopher Cicero. This was not so much a smart find as a lucky break, because for the most part the body of Celtic folk song has come into being through the efforts of some totally obsessed individuals.

A.W. Moore, for example, was so obsessed he set out to translate scores of Manx ballads, to the tune of an 1896 Anglicized collection, and if you've ever looked at the Manx language you'll applaud this. Another collector became so enamored with Germany's Grimm fairy tales, that nothing less than becoming the world authority on Scottish and English parallels would do. This was Francis Child, a transplanted American who eventually collected so many saucy, sordid and morbid songs he just had to number them all, and that's how they're usually known.

Cecil Sharp was another who took the road to obsession, and ended up most manically in the New World. Born in London, England, in 1859, he was a Cambridge-educated scholar and musicologist who even trained as a pianist, but didn't let it ruin him. Within that educated man was a wild heart and soul just aching to encapsulate the best in traditional folk song.

Cecil got quite turned on by a Morris dance, and began roaming his country for traditional tunes. He dabbled with Romany gypsy melodies, but then took ship for Appalachian America, where reams of Scots and Irish had headed in the 18th and 19th centuries. Cecil, who suffered from various disorders beyond Atlantic sea-sickness, had a real gut feeling that a lot of Celts in America had a lot of songs.

Bucked up by his faithful secretary, Maud Karpeles, he travelled by mule and buckboard through these wild regions. And though the determined duo ran up against fear, suspicion (of being German spies), bad-mouthing and buckshot, Cecil got his songs, and hundreds of them, having the most luck in the most broken-down areas. Those afflicted by poverty had had to learn to make their own songs or go without, just what Cecil was looking for.

He also believed in a kind of musical "natural selection" – that only the brightest and the best would be picked up and carried on – with, of course, some variants. Folk music wasn't a stagnant thing, after all. There usually was plenty of life beneath the pond, and that's why Cecil also meant to go to Newfoundland, Canada. He suspected there was a gold mine of seagoing balladry there, but died before he could do it. Maud went in his stead, a daring thing for women to do at that time. She trawled for shanty chants, and hauled up enough of them for a good book or two.

Maud would not be alone in female collective history here. Two noted 20th-century collectors were Canada's Edith Fowke and Helen Creighton. The former had plenty of field days throughout Canada, especially in Ontario and Quebec. The latter, from the 1930s on, trotted her melodeon around on a wheelbarrow through Nova Scotia, collecting ballads from the homelands, and funning things up with a few tunes on her melodious music-maker.

Both women ended up also collecting reams of what you might call Canadiana, but which inevitably had older links. This kind of detective work would make for some especially impressive volumes of Celtadian folk music.

A few words must be given here to the man who deserves perhaps the biggest bow from Celtic musicians today. You'll meet Francis O'Neill in Chapter 14, but for now, let's just say he ultimately put together one of the most impressive collections of trad music music ever, some time after he arrived in Chicago. He found himself just surrounded by the stuff, and there's nothing like getting away from the homeland to realize how meaningful it all is.

*

# Chapter 12

## Celtacholia — The Songs

One of the first things you'll find in digging around Celtic music history is total confusion. You get to know a song, then run into someone else singing different words to the same tune. Time and again, one melody, myriad sets of lyrics. *Rollin' in the Rye Grass,* for example, also is known as *The Lady's Top Dress, The Lady's Tight Dress, What the Divil Ails You?* and about four dozen other titles.

Another grainy song, *The Wind That Shakes the Barley,* is about the 1798 Irish uprising (and its 19th-century author was a Fenian rebel himself, who fled to America to hammer out Irish songs and ballads). But this popular pipe reel had an earlier incarnation with Robert Burns, who had used it as *Scots Wha' Hae' Wi' Wallace Bled,* which is what the movie *Braveheart* is all about. It also was Robert the Bruce's march, only then it started out as *Here Now the Day Dawns* – none of which explains why it's also called *Hey Tutti Tatti.*

In fact, songs took on enough identities to give any psychiatrist a challenge, but it's not really difficult to understand. As one song hit a region and stuck around, its words got changed to reflect regional likes and dislikes. An anthem became a nursery lullaby or nonsense song. Songs that traveled, or were misunderstood, misheard or misplaced, inevitably got changed. There also was some reincarnation and shape-shifting at work.

It also could work the other way, and a title become a magnet for melodies. There's a 27-verse Irish lament, *Is bronach mo thocht,* by 17th-century poet Seafraidh O Donnchadha. It's about the poet's pet spaniel, who was choked when a mouse being chased by a cat jumped into its mouth. This tale of tails became such a hit it coughed up enough tunes to equal its stanzas.

As for that perennial favourite *Danny Boy* to whom the "pipes are calling," people began arguing over whether the melody itself had come from: the *sidhe* folk of Irish legend, third-century Finn McCool, blind harpers Rory Dall Morrison, Rory Dall O'Cahan, Turlough O'Carolan, and Denis O'Hampsey, 19th-century blind fiddler Jimmy McCurry, or all of the above. And they're still at it.

*Danny* had picked up many different lyrics before it was so boyishly embraced, but English barrister Fred Weatherly scribbled away on a commuter train in 1910 to give us the ones we know. The melody itself is known as *Londonderry Air* by some, *London Derrière* by others. The whole thing has had a good run with the likes of Rosemary Clooney, tenor John McDermott, old-rockers Eric Clapton and Freddy Mercury, angst-filled youngster Sinead O'Connor, and it's not over yet.

As for who is actually singing to Danny within the song, well, author Malachy McCourt has tackled that question in his *Danny Boy: The Beloved Irish Ballad.* Right through a ten-down-to-number-one list, we're given a scholarly debate of contenders. Is it Danny's priest? His gay lover? His straight lover? Most likely ... it's dear old Mum.

The melancholia of leave-taking continues in songs like *The Irish Rover* and *Paddy's Green Shamrock Shore,* which describe the emigrants' Atlantic voyage in no un-certain times. But though it may have been no fun to travel that way, it was a *ceili* compared to what's behind *Black Velvet Band.* In this song, the usual sucker meets a dish with eyes like diamonds and hair tied up with, you guessed it, a black velvet band. They get all loopy together, then she slips a watch into his pocket at the market, he gets nabbed, and it's 10 years penal servitude.

This probably meant Van Dieman's Land (Tasmania), where one Lt. John Brown lovingly had established a British Empire incarceration colony in the early 1800s. Mere petty crime got you a place on the boat, and the whole thing caused untold misery to family and lovers, as well as the convicted. It didn't stop them songwriting, though, and this black armband became a public service offering, to beware of those colleens who'll get you drunk, deported and digging ditches far away.

In fact, women inspired a lot of songs. *The Rose of Tralee* was penned in the 1830s by one William Mulchinock, who fell for Mary O'Connor, a domestic in his home. Alas, it was one of those doomed affairs because Mary was a commoner, William born to a grand family.

They firmly extricated him from this thorny web, or so they thought. He came back from India in 1849, stopped in at a pub to freshen up before calling on Mary, and just out the door collided with a funeral cortege. Willie's complexion became nearly as deathly as Mary's, and his heart broke like a worn-out fiddle string.

He married someone else, moved to America, had a family, separated, put himself back together and came back home to drink himself right into a grave state. In the end, Willie was united with Mary in the same plot, and you could only hope they both got something out of it. Irish communities around the world certainly did, because a big annual festival has taken root from the song, and celebrants come from all over for the crowning of the Rose Queen.

*The Flowers of the Forest* has little to do with either flora or girls, and everything to do with the flower of manhood lost at battle. This famous lament came into being after the Scottish King James IV lost by a long shot to the English at the Battle of Flodden Field in 1513. Others insist the song was written to commemorate the equally disastrous Battle of Culloden in 1746. Flodden, Culloden, a sorry affair that represents what so often happened to the Scots.

Once you get everything translated in the version that's full of words like *Dowie* and *wae* (dismal and sad) *leglin* (an illegitimate child) *runkle* (wrinkle) *fleeching* (begging), *bogle* (a spectre or hobgoblin) *wede* (withered) and *dool* (grief), you can only conclude this is no party song.

And though there's no evidence that a local woman immediately put the whole sodden disaster immediately into song as in Celtic tradition, two later ladies a la moan, Jane Elliot and Alison Cockburn, did create lyrics. To this day, the song is performed at funerals, even those with no battles behind them.

*Loch Lomond* is another depressing song about the Scottish Jacobite cause. Jacobite, by the way, was a highfalutin name for those who followed the Stuarts, most named James, or *Jacobus* in Latin. In fact, the Jacobites actually believed their king's authority came from God, not Parliament, and this did not sit well with the English in command. Thus, clans were decimated, families destroyed, and tartans, weapons and music ripped from the people.

One of Bonnie Prince Charlie Stuart's soldiers scribbled down this number after the Culloden disaster, though couldn't do much with it, as he was executed. His pal-in-arms did get away, and took the song back to the dead soldier's sweetheart. The writer of the song says, or sings, that he will reach Scotland before his companion, because his spirit will travel by the "low road." Pass the *snoot-cloots* (handkerchiefs), if you please.

The story behind *MacPherson's Rant* starts out lively enough, because freewheeling fiddler Jimmy MacPherson was a career robber, rather like Robin Hood, only there's no mention of his helping the poor. He mostly saw to himself, carrying out a reign of terror in Scottish markets as he did so. Sentenced to be hanged for arms-bearing in November 1700, he had the prescience of mind to compose this song while waiting for the end, and they let him play it on the scaffold. But the audience had little patience for a musical interlude. They'd just come for the main show.

MacPherson, trying again, offered his fiddle to the crowd, but had no takers. He slammed it over his knee, tossed the pieces aside and snarled to the hangman, "Mither told me there'd be days like this, when naething goes right. But maybe some bugger will remember the melody and immortalize me!" Which is exactly what happened. He also inspired *MacPherson's Lament* and *Mac-Pherson's Farewell,* a body of song known as *The Three Terrors-and-Tears.*

*Auld Lang Syne* is not such a downer, though it does result in some hangovers, because it's usually sung on New Year's Eve. And as poet Robert Burns is responsible for it (though took it down from "an old man's singing"), it's a safe bet a lot of his inspiration came from Scotch, which also may be why Burns' publisher rejected its original tune as "not quite right for us." That Burns was fixated on partying can be seen in Auld lyrics like "a cup of kindness," as well as in other Burnt offerings, that describe Scotch drinking, drinking to one's health, a tippling ballad, and the address of Beelzebub.

*Scotland The Brave*, also known as *Road to the Isles,* is pretty self-explanatory, and though it's usually played instrumentally, it has some rousing verses to match the melody. At last, something upbeat to remember Scotland by. Unfortunately, there's next to no information about this song, and that's probably why.

Scotland's cousin Wales has a few songs that reached world vernacular, and one of those is *The Ash Grove.* It's another of those multiple-personality pieces of music, also known as *Sir William Watkin Wynn, The Master Has Come, The Irish Free State,* and in a mangled way as *Constant Billy,* and *Cease Your Funning* from John Gay's 1728 *The Beggar Opera.* Originally, it was a harp melody, so it's no wonder so many composters harped on it.

Many a harp has plunked *All Through the Night* or *Ar Hyd Y Nos,* another Welsh keeper, equally good as lullaby and church song. It first appeared in the 1780s *Musical Relics of the Welsh Bards,* then got lyricized by 19th-century railway manager John Hughes. Just in case anyone doubted he was only playing at being poet, he put together five volumes of Welsh poetry, and gave himself a bardic title, Glyn Ceiriog, after the name of his home valley.

*All Through Seven Years* was the alternate title for what's become Wales's national anthem, the rousing *Men of Harlech.* Harlech Castle got roped into the War of the Roses in the 1400s, when forces under the castle's Welsh constable, Dafydd ap Jevan, defended the digs for the Lancastrians (the red-rose crowd).

After a seven-year holdout, Dafydd, a shadow of his former self, handed over the key to the invaders. White-rose King Edward IV first refused the honorable terms, but Sir Richard Herbert of Edward's army said he'd die rather than see the promise broken. That's how highly he thought of these defenders, and it's the kind of stuff that just has to be sung up.

Possibly, the tune was composed by Edward's chief harper, but in any case, it showed up in a 1784 volume *Musical and Poetical Relicks of the Welsh Bards.* The words to the song, *Gwyr Harlech* in Welsh, were penned by John "Ceiriog" Hughes, that 19th-century poet who went at it all through the night, while one John Oxenford took time out from writing 68 plays and translating Molière and Goethe, to Anglicize this little Celtic project.

Old Irish song *Droimeann Donn Dilis* – about a cow that represents Ireland – got well-Anglicized in its travels.

It was shortened in America to *Poor Drimmer*, then early 20th-century black musician Leadbelly moseyed around with the melody, then folksinger Pete Seeger embraced it as *Kisses Sweeter Than Wine* in the 1950s, and people are still smooching it about. *Groyle Machree* (bastardization of *Gradh Geal Mo Cridhe* or "bright heart's love") left Ireland to travel through the American Ozark Mountains, then up into Ontario and Nova Scotian versions in Canada. And as it's about doomed love and a willow tree, it just wept all the way.

The arboreal angst theme continues with Galicia's winning entry, its anthem. Taken from poet Eduardo Pondal's piece *Os Pinos* (The Pines) this separatist song is called *Fogar de Breogan* (Home of Breogan). The song gently needles Breogan, the ancient king, to wake up and listen to the wind in the trees, which really is the hot air of those so-often-suppressed Galicians. All along it was frowned upon by Spanish powers-that-be, so it had to get going somewhere else. That was in Havana, Cuba in 1907, and it was the whole emigration experience that brought this song, like Galicia's flag and coat-of-arms, into being.

*Arrane Ashoonagh Dy Vannin* or *Land of our Birth* is probably not one you'll hear any time soon, unless you're on the Isle of Man. Though it's actually set to the tune of *Mylecharaine,* a story about a miser and his daughter's dowry, overall it's a piece that moves the Manx very deeply (in spite of the fact it was written by an Englishman born in Sicily). It's sometimes called their national air, which is rather nationalistic, but the oldest self-governing nation of the Celtic world is allowed some airs.

When the modern Manx were polled about the song that should carry this honour, results brought in *God Save The Queen* at 7% (the Manx do recognize her, if not British Parliament), *Ellan Vannin* (a revamped old folk song the Manx-born Bee Gee brothers have maxed out in London's Wembley Stadium) at 23%, and *Land of Our Birth* at 59%.

Both homeland and plants figure in *The Maple Leaf Forever*. Scotsman Alexander Muir, who arrived in Toronto in 1833 to schoolteach and moonlight as Canada's very own Robbie Burns, wrote it as the country's big Confederation hit for 1867. He was out having an autumnal stroll, a maple leaf came down to land on his sleeve and kept sticking, and he promptly stuck together a song whose lyrics (tampered with over the years) also would play up, amongst other plants, the thistle and shamrock for Scotland and Ireland.

This floral theme would go on to present itself in the Canadian coat-of-arms' crest as symbols of some of the founding nations of Canada. You go, Celts. And that brings us to the next chapter.

*

## Chapter 13

# Come West, Young Celt — Oh, Canada!

A lot of songs came over to the New World, and earlier than you may think.

Sixth-century St. Brendan the Navigator reached a far-western land of Celtic legend and saw enough sea monsters on the way to touch down with lots of material (as well as inspire 1970s Tim Severin the reNavigator to follow in his footsteps, then write a book called *The Brendan Voyage*). Other seafaring ancient Celts pushed inland to Peterborough, Ontario, where they fought with native Canadians to inscribe some script on boulders. Eighth-century Scottish exiles and ninth-century Culdee monks also came chanting over the waters.

Then Scottish Prince Henry Sinclair hit Nova Scotia in 1398, with several boatloads of knights and bards, and also got sucked up into the province's Mi'k Maq (MicMac)-native great-white-mythman Glooscap legend. Unbeatable song material.

But even if orthodox historians don't buy all this, they'd probably agree that centuries ago Breton fishermen came over around to net around Newfoundland, and it's difficult to believe they would have done it without a few songs to keep them going. We do know that some Scots came to "New Scotland," Nova Scotia, in the early 1600s, until they got chased out by the British-pursued French, the Acadians.

When the Scots tried next, after the 18th-century Battle of Culloden and its fallout, they did better. "Better" is a relative word. They'd been brutally cleared out of the Highlands and their whole way of life and language destroyed. All that and the Atlantic voyage, as well as scrabbling to survive in a new place, made for a depressing scenario, but also for some memorable songs after the fact.

Some were filled with references to clansmen, claymores and exile, and hearts left behind in the Highlands. *Oran do'n chuair tear* (A Song for the Tourist), extolled the virtues of the Highlander, from cross-tied garters to sword and dirk, and proclaimed that Gaelic was the language of Adam, no less. Still, this new land had a certain resemblance to home.

The earliest Gaelic song composed in Cape Breton seems to be *Baile Na Traghad* (My Home on the Seashore), which rolled out around 1775 from Michael Mor MacDonald. Michael had been a well-known bard back in Scotland, so he milked Celtic themes to include cows, salmon, piping and fiddling in the song, and it's a surprisingly upbeat piece.

*The Gloomy Forest* was an 1820, 18-verse effort by John Maclean, who had come to the new land all pumped up to be a grand estate lord, but just got lost in the woods. When he found his way out, he put his kids to work while he barded away, trying to create a local Gaelic arts scene. *Am Mealladh* or *The Deception* also summed up John's thoughts on the new land.

John, "the Hunter" MacDonald (1795-1853) contributed *Geamhradh an t-sneachda mhoir* (Winter of the Big Snow), to add to an anonymous Maclean bard's *Gearainair America* or *Complaint About America*. Other chart-topplers like *How Sorrowful I Am*, *The Song of Hard Times*, and *My Heart Is Sad*, had all the joy of sick bagpipes at their lowest drone.

Occasionally people were able to put all this aside, and fiddle up some of the happier stuff of Scottish composers like Niel Gow and Simon Fraser. And the later

Canadian song *Trip to Mabou Ridge* was a prophetic one, because some time after, Mabou would become a show-stopping name in Nova Scotian trad-Celtic music production.

For a lot of Scots who came out in the 18th and early 19th centuries "making music" also meant going to someone's house for a few gallons of Jamaica rum, which somehow got through Canada's own Prohibition. Other entrepreneurs made the song *Good Health to the Moon-shiners* a popular and patriotic one. Musical kitchen parties in Nova Scotia were fun, fun, fun. Those partiers who could do the whole Gaelic histrionics show were especially popular. Things would get really competitive, till everyone had run out of voice, rhyme or rum. The kitchen party would prove to be a long-lasting Nova Scotian affair.

Those hooked on preaching, though, were really convinced about the demon rum factor, and with them, songs of Daffydd might get replaced by Psalms of David. But even that became just another element in a good mix. The Irish and Scottish were already mixing and matching their numbers from sung-up to sundown (and it was the Irish, you remember, who first made Scotland what it was). And all along the coast, Scots mingled with Swiss and French so there were plenty of holey *chansons* just full of Scotch.

In those old New-Scotland days, blind pipers and fiddlers, as well as their progeny, made music amidst a porridge pot of musical stock like Black Angus, Black Angus McFarlane, Angus Johnnie, Big Farquhar and Little Farquhar McKinnon. As for the MacCrimmon clan back in Scotland of yore, their airs must have been burning, because the "great music," *piobaireachd,* was shunned in favour of marches, reels, strathspeys and other get-down stuff here in Canada.

Cape Breton's own potato blight in the 1840s put a halt to the streams of Scots and Irish coming over, so the population settled down. By that time, though, there were enough songs to run with, and the music scene in Cape Breton just got bigger and bigger, as well as smaller and smaller. Babies were sung to sleep and sung awake, learned how to hold a fiddle before a nipple and to step-dance before they walked.

Any other newcomers arrived in a spirit of some adventure rather than desperation, and to communities that were not only settled, but full of *ceilidhs*, *craic* and *ri-ra*. The newly formed New Brunswick also welcomed Irish, Scottish and Welsh loyalists from the U.S., and someone on a dark night invented the Black Watch Regiment, which would be blamed for a lot of organized piping, in that province and beyond.

In the 1930s there were two events of real note. Immigrant Angus MacKenzie put everybody's enthusiasms into the Gaelic College of Celtic Arts at St. Ann's, Nova Scotia, and one Rev. John Campbell went mechanical, and started recording songs. Many waxed rapturous over his wax-cylinder machine. Not only did he get down "the Gaelic," he also got down some indigenous M'ik Maq language, believed to be the first so captured. There was something akin in the rhythms, and if 14th-century Prince Henry Sinclair of Scotland really was the Glooscap hero of Micmac legend, it had been going on for some time.

The Irish, whether medieval sailors, monks or later musical travellers, preferred Newfoundland, because it was a big island, just like back home. Water Street, in Newfoundland's capital city St. John's, was the oldest shopping strip (c.1498 CE) in the New World, so it was already used to buskers. The region got known for a well-musselled mélange of folk music. Welsh, Bretons and Scots also liked Newfoundland, and in the end, nearly everyone could appreciate that most famous of Newfie songs, *I'se The B'y* even though it's full of new-regional references like Bonavista, Twillingate Harbour, and the cod that encompasses.

Tiny Prince Edward Island got boatloads of Scottish immigrants with fiddlers galore, and the Irish brought more with them, mixing it up with some French-Acadian holdouts. The fiddling scene became a regionally incriminating one that defied counting all the styles, as well as denied women. Then came the P.E.I. suffragette movement in the 1930s, when some fretting sisters fought for the right to fiddle, and in public, for the dances. It caused some mighty staccato, but eventually enough menfolk remembered that historically speaking, women did a lot of important song-work in keeping things alive, so just as long as the girls remembered to cook, clean and procreate, they were allowed.

PEI-ers went especially for the reels – *St. Anne's Reel*, *Lord MacDonald's Reel*, *The Princess Reel*. Home-away favourite *Miss Scott* became *The Indian Reel*, and islanders also were far-sighted enough to go for *The Ottawa Valley Reel* and *Jerome's Farewell to Gibraltar*.

Those Celts who didn't stop-off-and-stay on the East Coast continued inland, some heading for the U.S. A lot of Irish ended up in Quebec in the 1830s & '40s, not because they wanted to, but because coffin ships full of cholera and typhus got them quarantined or buried at Grosse Isle.

This scenario periodically put a real damper on composition, but in spite of it all, the Irish never stopped making music. Quebec became known for its *eires, aers,* jigs and reels, as well as Irish-Scotch *scoradatura* techniques, where you fiddle around with the strings to create sympathetic vibrations. Some people, though, had no sympathy at all for this, or even less for the music a minor invasion of Celts from Brittany brought over.

In Quebec, there also were some interesting exchanges between European explorers and Canadian aboriginals. Gaelic hymns and fiddling around in general charmed the local Cree population, and in Quebec-Inuit territories, those jigs and reels moved with little trouble into things like *Eskimo Dance.* But all of this pales in comparison to the impression the bagpipes made on the indigenous population. Most were awestruck at the sight of men in colored skirts and whooping it up into the mouths of birds, and there was immediate competition in turning this weaponry to their advantage.

Other pipes wailed, along with fiddles, down into Ontario. The Celts retained their wood-be obsessions with plenty of Irish, Scottish and Canadian ballads about life in the big forest. Many songs had to do with two major Irish-Canadian issues, the lumber industry and the unemployment scenario, and often the twain met. But though No Irish Need Apply was a sign of the times, many of these loose solo singers laid on the accents for defiance' sake. They also borrowed songs from the coast, like *Banks of Newfoundland* to add to their catch of Lake Ontario sailor songs.

Meanwhile, other folk headed far west to God-for-saken places like Assiniboia and Saskatchewan. Pipers and bards, with a few females among them, found their songs about Scottish moors on a May morning giving way to more hurtin' songs about Canadian winters.

The 19th-century Scottish bard John MacLean's *Song For Manitoba*, in Gaelic *Oran do Mhanitoba,* proclaimed that this forbidding land would yet have a "MacLean's Hill." The song made even more of the fact that though he and the folks may have complained about their prospects on New Year's Eve last year at home, out here they really had every reason to do so.

Others headed for Dakota across the border, where they thought things would be better, but mid-1880s depression and poverty there merely made for songs so depressing they had to come back to Canada. Some headed further west, to sing down Vancouver, or *Bhancouver,* as it was known. Overall, people tried to remain upbeat with fun songs like *Song to the Moccasin, Song to the Broken Fiddle* and *Song to my Breaking Back.* Others just kept going west, to Australia and New Zealand, with a lot of travel time to make up tunes.

Fur-traders who hailed from Scotland, Ireland and French Canada from the 1600s on blew on their frozen fingers all the way over and up to the Northwest and Yukon Territories. Here, again, those fiddling rhythms, once the hands were thawed, managed to find some meeting place with indigenous merry-making. The Athabascan natives came up with *Red River Jig* (Jig Ahtsii Ch'aadzaa). *Rabbit Dance* and *Duck Dance* (an early version of *The Bird Dance*) were big hits, while *Devil's Dream* was a diabolic standard in both cultures.

Gold-rush-influenced music, like jigs-to-the-mother-lode, added luster, and someone looking for nuggets also came up with inspirational songs like *In the Mode for a Lode* and *Vein Glories*. The gold of roots music or heavy metal, it all was part of the Celtic-Canada mettle that carved out new homelands.

Things got heavy in the 1860s, too, with some less-than-Civil musical input, courtesy of some neo-Fenians south of the border. Modern Irish revolutionaries who fed on tales of Finn McCool and the nasty English iron hand decided to invade Canada, to force Britain to give Ireland her freedom. About 200,000 Fens gathered, and there were melees around Niagara and Toronto, that did go their way. They celebrated with on-the-spot variations of their on-the-spot *A Fenian Song*.

They were not to sing for long, because fightin' mad Canadians drove back successive waves of them, and their own U.S. government nabbed the leaders. The Canadians followed things right up with their own Anti-Fenian song, set to the American Civil War melody of *Tramp, Tramp, Tramp, the Boys Are Marching*.

And they marched right into the 20th century, where, with or without wars looming in the background, the music continued to grow. Don Messer came out of a New Brunswick family of 11 kids to pick up a fiddle and star in a downhome radio program presenting "Canadian folk music," flavoured with both Irish and Scotch. CBC TV thought enough of him to began running his *Jubilee* program in the 1950s.

Considered the Canadian equivalent of *The Ed Sullivan Show,* it was filled with interesting characters like musical "Islanders," Charlie Chamberlain-the-lumber-jack, and a character named Duke Neilsen, who played 22 musical instruments and was a bear-wrestler and fire-eater to boot. When the show was cancelled, people dried their tears enough to erect a giant fiddle to Don in Harvey, New Bunswick.

In the meantime, Newfoundland's Harry Hibbs pounded out jigs, reels and ballads on accordion, in his own Scottish-and-Irish meets country-and-western mix. Another show was born, and they kept coming, from *Singalong Jubilee* to *The Pig and Whistle.*

And by the 1960s, a reworked version of American Woody Guthrie's *This Land Is Your Land*, with Canadian-specific lyrics, was hailed as the ultimate Celtadian song. After all, what would Canada have been without all those Celts making waves? It was they who had settled from Bonavista (Newfoundland), to Vancouver Island. From sea to sea and from C to C, they had sung, fiddled, dreamed and droned a new land into existence.

\*

# Chapter 14

# Come West, Young Celt: Americay!

Just exactly when the Celts first came to America is equally open to question. Sometimes they got mixed up and went to Armorica (Brittany) instead.

There's some support for Celtic Prince Madoc ap Rhys Owen, who hit the Atlantic with a boatload of sickness-and-Welsh in 1170. He landed in the southeast U.S., and worked his way inland, while his minstrel William the Flem continued to embroider a tale of his employer finding a new kingdom, of "eternal youth, love and music" in the sun. Madoc and his men supposedly intermarried with America's Mandan tribes, so it's possible a new beat was born then.

But Madoc or not, a few centuries after that, America beckoned oversea-ers as the land of opportunity, for poor and better-off emigrants alike. Occasionally it was because *My Love Is In America* (or "Americay," as it was called, in hopes of some cracking *ceilis* there), and in that case you were glad to go. Still, leavetaking, for leavetakers and homestayers alike, proved to be such a wrench people could only work it out by whooping it up, in one last grand, "may the circle never be unbroken" kind of get-together.

This idea gets electrifying treatment in the *Riverdance* segment *American Wake*. However, though 18th- and 19th-century Celts in Ireland and Scotland may not have had farewell orchestras and full makeup, they were showy enough with fiddles, flutes and feets. Then they sobered up enough to light their hearths from those of the leave-takers, so the circle would remain an unbroken ring of fire as well.

Galicians and Asturians who came over headed right for New York, or for spicier South America, Mexico and Havana, Cuba. In fact, here the Gallego language would at last find the welcome home it had been pining for for years. The Havana Real Academia Galega, founded in 1905, laid down the standardization it was just too dicey to attempt in the homeland.

Some Celts headed west to California. The song-making that came out of that movement ranged from joyful ("it's so warm and dry here!") to confused ("it's so warm and dry here"). The Californians already there were considered "loose" and "soft," so were good subjects for any number of *aels, aers* and *flytings*. Many Irish and Scots adapted quite happily, though, to life in a gold climate, and as you can see in Hollywood today, they're still doing it.

Most Celts spread themselves out over the Appalachian mountain lands of Kentucky, the Virginias, the Carolinas and Tennessee. Many Scots felt debatably at home, as the Appalachians were joined to the Highlands before the Atlantic Ocean came between them. Still, there was a lot of minor-mode stuff and (miner as well, as the Welsh had come over to work the hills), and a lot of pining for the homeland trees. However, the hit *Oran America* (Song to America) indicates they were able to stop weeping long enough to get on with things.

And when the going gets tough, the Celts get dancing, and they just did it all up and down the coast and in the hills, with from-the-homelands stepdancing that turned into clog dancing and square dancing. Many settlers happily adapted the Scottish *muckle sang* ballads to new surroundings, but with pretty well the same old themes of love, lust, labor, loss, larceny, mistaken identity, murer, and even worse, absence of whiskey.

The enterprising ones got together in the evenings, and figured out how to make moonshine, and lesser-known Celtic-American ballads like *In Our Still of the Night*, *Brewhaha* and *Shine's On!* were brewed. It was a nice link with their entrepreneurial Gaelic ancestors, some of whom had stopped lamenting long enough to make *poitin*, or poteen. Some settlers had strong ideas about salvation, damnation and drink, but with others, the idea that the devil might be behind both drink and music livened things up.

However, there was a lot of church singing that came out of the Appalachians, and sometimes it melded quite nicely with old ballads. One that everyone seemed to like was an old Hebridean waulking song called *A' Bhratach Breacadh Nan Reult*, which translates to *The Star Spangled Banner*. Add this to the Irish insistence that Turlough O'Carolan wrote the melody for this new land's national anthem, and you'll see how Celtic America really is.

There were few harps, but there was the mountain dulcimer, that twangy little Scottish-European-inspired instrument that took shape one day in the Appalachians. The dulcimer had enough of a gentle drone to recall the pipes of home. With it, couples were courted, babies comforted, hymns elaborated upon, and as it spun out a mean *caoineadh* it also was music to die for. One family, the "Singing Ritchies" of Viper, Kentucky, would produce a balladeer called Jean who would bring the dulcimer to worldwide fame.

In America as at home, it was not considered good form for musicians to get any sort of "training." That just muddied up that pure-as-mountain-spring-moonshine music, and didn't go with the clannishness, feuding and strong accents just as at home in these Highlands.

Scottish freedom fighters, and drovers who had herded homeland Highland cattle to lowland tryst markets did some shape-shifting to become cowboys and cattle ranchers. Jigs and songs assumed new identities. *The Bard of Armagh*, about an old harper whose fingers can't harp anymore so it's time to die, became *The Streets of Laredo*. Now its subject was a good-looking gambler who found that pride, as well as syphilis and a gunshot in the chest, was his fall.

The competitive spirit that was beginning to make America what it was also fuelled big fiddling festivals, often helped along by early-auto magnate Henry Ford. Hank adored Appalachian music, and when he wasn't wheeling around, was reeling around, with the where-withal to donate pots of money for old-time fiddling contests. If you got really lucky, you might even be invited to play at his summer home.

Unfortunately, if you were Irish, you often went back to a less-than-stellar life, in cities like New York, Chicago and Boston. Some suffered this discrimination with even more whiskey than usual, others created the American Catholic Church, others just made music about it, and in certain circles it became a bit of a cult thing to be Irish. Songwriter Stephen Foster made much of the fact his great-grandfather had come from Derry in the 1720s, but others much closer to the greenery made plenty of noise about it.

One of these was Francis O'Neill. Francis, who was good with a flute, was born during the 1840s Irish Potato Famine, where he came to thrill to the occasional "This spud's for you." He somehow found the strength to become a shepherd, a teacher, and shipwrecked, all in all a terrific start for songwriting. Fury at his homeland priest who had banned public dances and forced a local piper into the poorhouse, fired his determination to keep the music alive, even if he had to get seasick and come to America to do it.

Paying no attention to that "No Irish Need Apply" stuff, he became not only a cop but a superintendent of the Chicago police, which gave him some say-so in most things. In his spare time, he fluted, tooted, and started hanging around Irish musicians, forming sessions and scribbling lots of notes.

And then one day someone said to Francis, "O'Neill, meet O'Neill." James O'Neill was a young fiddler who could read and write music, and who promptly got a job in Francis's cop shop, as did lots of other trad musicians who needed a good financial base. "May the Force be with you," musicians would solemnly say to each other as they began tuning up in musical sessions.

In their offtime, Francis and James began collecting loads and modes of folk music, and there was plenty to find in America. The immigrants made more of their songs here than back home. Jimmy was good on the business end of it, too. He did consumer market surveys, trying to get a finished product that pleased most of the people. The ultimate O'Neills' compilation, which appeared in 1903, comprised over 1850 pieces, including 1,100 dance tunes.

In comparison, Irish collectors Ed Bunting and George Petrie had embarrassingly small numbers of these. Leave it to a couple of Chicago cops to do better in their spare time. And Bunting and Petrie really were antiquarian scholars dressing up the whole thing for a middle-class audience. The O'Neills were doing it for "just folk," of whom they were two.

Their collection became something simply called "The Book," mainstay of many a modern Celtic musician's repertory. Amongst the jigs, reels and airs, there's plenty of O'Carolan stuff and a lot of songs like *Barney O'Neill, Mary O'Neill, Young Edmond O'Neill, Shane O'Neill's March, Captain O'Neill's Visit*, and *Superintendent O'Neill's Overkill*. Other books followed, the charming *Gaelic Waifs and Strays* dedicated to the city's shapeshifting animal overpopulation.

As Francis and Jimmy's efforts went into overdrive, the uillean pipes were being beefed up by two Irish brothers named Taylor, who'd come over to America to promptly modify the instrument's chanter bore, not to make it boring, but to make it louder. This kind of thing, musicians found, was taylor-made for the bigger audiences and bigger spaces here.

And the time was ripe for The Golden Age of Irish Americanism, a nostalgic effort equally soaked in tipples and tears. *I'll Take You Home Again Kathleen* and *Galway Bay*, *Mother Machree* and *When Irish Eyes Are Smiling*, were songs the folks back home wouldn't have known, though they were sung up aplenty by the likes of Irish-in-America tenor John McCormack. *Who Threw the Overalls in Mrs. Murphy's Chowder?* was the theme song that in Irish Music Hall and other halls of infamy treated the Irishman as a love-him-hate-him buffoon.

This viscous vocal output began to clog up Tin Pan Alley, the music-publishing biz around New York's 28th Street, and would stick around to clog North American perceptions for decades. As time went on, though, the Irishman increasingly was considered a resourceful fellow, and one reason was that the Saint Patrick he'd brought over became excellent for American industry. St. Pat was big in Church, taverns and parades, and it all became the greening of the tourist industry.

Things got differently colored, when Irish musicians became early blackface minstrels, and entertainer Thomas Dartmouth "Daddy" Rice joined his own African-American shuffle dance with an Irish fiddle tune. Somehow it all worked, and out of it came big minstrel dance tunes like *Jimmy Crack Corn, Jump Jim Crow* and *Jimmy Pops Corn*.

Both black and Irish cultures had catchy rhythms, liked simple scales and dancing to vocals, and both also exhibited a certain nasality, due partly to those infectious steerage quarters. As well, both cultures wanted something better out of life, and music helped.

This idea of this kind of musical meeting-matching-and-mixing has resulted in *Riverdance* highlight *Trading*

*Taps*, where Irish high-steppers compete with Harlem shufflers-cum-gymnasts. They antagonize and ape each other, until they're all in sync at the end, and racial harmony wins out. The *Riverdance* segment *Harbour of the New World* simply tried to cover as many races as it could.

In any case, after 1900, The Gaelic League in America started encouraging people to dance together in groups, and musicians were always needed. Drone-throners like Patsy Touhey blew Vaudeville away, and thanks to the Taylor brothers' tinkering, everyone heard them. The patronage system also lived again, as some lucky pipers got themselves sponsored for around $200 a year.

As for Irish fiddlers in America in the 1920s, there were none better than County Sligo boys James Morrison and Michael Coleman. James dedicated *Wheels of the World* to Henry Ford, and Michael spun out *The Sailor's Bonnet* and *Bonnie Kate* so magically people considered him a *sidhe* instead of a he.

Recording and radio also were changing trad music. Touhey, Coleman, Morrison and others went sailing back over, this time on new 78 rpm records, along with the Victrola gramophones to play them. It made for some electrifying new *seisiuns*. These kinds of recordings also eventually would take on the black-gold luster of American roots-records companies.

Meanwhile, that "high lonesome sound" hied its way right into a form of Americana known for its cash-register whine quotient, country music. The Celtic rhythms were a good start, but then you'd add a shuffle, a backbeat, even more depression, and there you were. Immigrants might still sing of the crofts they left behind, but their new home on the range was taking over. It also inspired one of the whiniest songs of all time, as the highland cow was reincarnated as the buffalo.

Country singer Jimmie Rodgers rode all the way into the spotlight with songs about love, loss and illness, about 20 million moaning discs of them by 1933. The

Bluegrass Boys, headed by Bill Monroe, with synchronized smart suits and harmonies, gave us the very term "bluegrass." They mixed *Roanoke* with *Scotland* in the repertoire, but whether or not bluegrass singing really is a descendent of Highland psalm singing still is open for debate.

Louder fiddles, banjos, mandolins, guitars, and oddities like the autoharp (a Celto-Germanic mixup like the mountain dulcimer) helped it all along. Musicians Johnny Cash and June Carter found common chords for a long-running marriage of notes, while singer Glen Campbell was a *Rhinestone Cowboy.*

Neo-traditionalist Ricky Skaggs took over from Bill Monroe as the official ambassador of bluegrass, and sowed the field with Celtic clues like *Ancient Tones* and *Connemara.* Recognition of country music's true roots watered a new transatlantic scene, as warblers, strummers and stringers from both sides of the ocean began playing around together.

In the Appalachian-meets-Erin LP *Another Country* (1992), Irish folk group The Chieftains scooped up American musicians Willie Nelson, Emmylou Harris, Chet Atkins and others seeking their shamrock-shore roots, aboard *The Wabash Cannonball,* stopping off for a mix of *Father Kelly's Reels* and *Cotton-Eyed Joe,* and asking *Did You Ever Go A-Courtin' Uncle Joe?*

The Chieftains would continue to go courting with country crooners, and their performances on *Down The Old Plank Road: The Nashville Sessions* (2002) and *Further Down The Old Plank Road* (2003), with Ricky Skaggs, Earl Scruggs, and many *mhor* prove that the Irish green grass-American bluegrass hybridization has not merely sprouted. It's been fertilized more richly than anyone could have for-scene.

*

# Chapter 15

# Classi — Celts

About the same time the Celts were bringing their music to North America, there were some interesting Celtural influences happening in, of all things, classical music.

Henry Purcell (1659-95) was one of the first to dabble. This chorister, court violin composer, abbey organist and harp player to James II, did a theatrical suite called *King Arthur*, in which numbers about trumpet tunes, warlike consorts and *No Part of my Dominion* got some light relief with a hornpipe.

Next up was 18th-century James Oswald, the Orpheus of the Scottish Violincello. He did collections of *Curious Scots Tunes*, and happily slapped together classical and folk by churning out nearly 100 Italian-style sonatas all based on traditional tunes, and named after British trees and flora.

In keeping with the nature theme, we must mention Dublin-born John Field (1782-1837). Though he invented the nocturne later plagiarized by Chopin, and Franz Liszt had a Field day publishing John's compositions, John was more welcome to the folks back home when he was playing old Irish airs like *Go and Shake Yourself*. This, after all, went back to everyone's Keltoi ancestors rising up out of the waters to conquer the world.

Scotland's Alexander Campbell MacKenzie (1847-1935) also had a Classical mis-start. His dad, Alexander MacKenzie, principal violinist/bandleader at Edinburgh's

Theatre Royal, sent little Alex to Germany to bow with Liszt, and Alex came back to nab the highly coveted King's Scholarship, teach, moonlight in chamber music orchestras, and lead bigger ones. But damn it, he was a Celt.

He created a classical *pibroch* (based on the Scottish bagpipe's "great music") in a few days, and other works like *Rhapsodie Ecossaise,* a Scotch Rhapsody to Burns, *Three Scottish Rhapsodies, Scottish Concerto,* and *The Caprice,* variations based on an old Scottish melody about Three Guid Fellows. Internationally-renowned violinist Pablo de Sarasate thought so highly of Alex's *Pibroch* he played it himself, and Alex dedicated a further work, *The Highland Ballad,* to his pal.

Anglo eccentric Granville Ransome Bantock also wandered into the Scottish playing field, but not before harping on Cyprian, Sapphoan, French, Chinese and Persian antiquity themes. Exhausted by such exoticism, he turned to his friend, Scottish collector Marjorie Kennedy-Fraser, and happily dipped into her store to produce his takes on a Hebridean symphony, a Celtic symphony, pieces about sea reivers and seal-women, a couple of heroic ballads, a *few Scottish Scenes from the Scottish Highlands*, a Scottish rhapsody, a coronach, a Scottish poem, a Celtic poem, plenty of *Sea Sorrow*, and a good old *pibroch* (for cello-and-harp-or-piano).

As for English composer Arnold Bax, he got bitten by the Celtic bug because right from his birth in 1883, home might be Glencolumcille, Ireland one week, Morar, Scotland the next. It was Ireland that really did it. Granville obsessed about faeries, learned Irish Gaelic, named his kids Dermot and Maeve, and wrote short stories as "Dermot O'Byrne."

He tried an opera around legendary lady Dierdre of the Sorrows, sorrowfully concluded it wasn't meant to be with an *Irish Elegy*, then cycled around with Irish tone poems *Eire,* traveling In *The Garden of Fand* and

*In the Faery Hills* right on *Into the Twilight,* stopping off for a *Roscatha* ("battle hymn" in Irish Gaelic), and a more successful female dalliance with *Cathaleen-ni-Hoolihan.*

A brilliant pianist, he was too shy to do anything about it in public, though not too shy to carry on a torrid affair after his marriage, with fellow pianist Harriet Cohen. It was while things were at their hottest between them that he wrote his masterpiece, the orchestral tone poem *Tintagel.*

Tintagel, a castle locale on the north coast of Cornwall, supposedly housed the illicit passion that led to King Arthur's birth, and doomed Arthurianites Tristan and Isolde also made out here. Bax panted away to musically evoke a classical lay by this legendary Atlantic landmark, lushing it up with late-Romantica, and full orchestra with woodwind, strings, harp and celesta, a small piano that thinks it's a glockenspiel. Sir Edward Elgar also felt enough *Pomp and Circumstance* to compose a body of incidental music about King Arthur and his hangers-on.

Edward's peer Ralph Vaughan Williams also remained largely English in his musical meanderings, but did wet his feet in the Celtic pool of plenty with an opera about Thomas the Rhymer, and instrumental pieces like *Five Variants of Dives and Lazarus.* Somehow, these rich-man-and-beggar New Testament, Book of Luke characters had become entangled with the melody of an old Irish piece, *The Star of the Country Down.*

Though "Rafe," as he was known, would create any number of folked-around orchestral situations (and could afford to go out looking for folk stuff, as he was descended from Wedgwoods and Darwins), he would cling to this Dives-and-Lazarus-do-the-county-down tune for the rest of his life. He pushed it into myriad choral scenarios and used it as theme in the *Festival Te Deum,* written for King George VI's coronation.

One of Ralph's biggest fans was Sir Adrian Boult, who dove right into *Dives* by conducting its first performance with the New York Philharmonic in 1939. The piece also marked Ralph's grand sendoff at Westminster Abbey in 1958, and never did it sound more heavenly.

Gustav Holst (1874-1934) was sucked up by planettary influences long before he died, as his most famous music shows, but he did put on *Seven Scottish Airs* and a treatment of Purcell's *King Arthur*. Gustav starts off his famous *St. Paul's Suite* with a jig, occasionally combined his interests in pieces like *Nocturne and Jig*, and touched down in Northumbria, that Celtic pocket of England improper, to do more rotating and notating before going back to ponder on the two planets he hadn't yet written music for.

A lot of European performers also were bitten by the Celtic music bug, and as the Keltoi did whoop and holler all over the European continent, this isn't so surprising. Handel broke new wind by using bagpipes, Bach got himself into a real *Fiddle Fugue*, Debussy did an *Iberia* suite, then a grand *March Ecossaise,* and Jean-Baptiste Lully and Joseph Haydn cranked up the hurdy-gurdy.

It was Felix Mendelssohn (1809-47) who would give the whole thing a star quality. Yes, he was an active propagandist for the neglected music of Bach, and quite active at home as a composer, pianist and organist, but then he got this itch to sail over to Britain to get in touch with some Celtic routes. Felix panted around after Sir Walter Scott and other poetic misjustices.

Then, after hitting Tobermory, the island of Iona and the island of Staffa with ancient Ossian hotspot Fingal's Cave, he stopped, closed his eyes, and cried out "I feel an overture coming on!" He couldn't resist writing to his family about this creative frenzy, and just in case they thought he was wasting his time and drinking whiskey, he enclosed the overture's opening bars in the letter. What resulted was his great *Hebrides* masterpiece, and though it has the Continental feel of a good sonata, it has enough great Scot in it to bring tears to the ayes.

Though the great Richard Wagner didn't like Felix, he did like his work and was man enough to say so. Brahms simply said, "I wish I had written it," though he did write his own *Gesang aus Fingal* (Song From Fingal).

Max Bruch (1838-1920) was fond enough of his native Germany, but started digging around one day in *The Scots Musical Museum*, an anthology collected by one James Johnson. He found a melody he liked, and it became his *Scottish Fantasy*, the stage name for *Fantasy for Violin and Orchestra and Harp freely using Scottish Folk Melodies, in E-flat Major, Op. 46*. It annoyed Max when people got the long form down wrong, but that usually was due to bad Scotch.

Beethoven periodically mixed his usual angry melancholy with some stirring Celtacholia, and did harmonizations of umpteen *Scottische, Welsche and Irische,* especially *Scottische, "lieders."* These songs paid tribute to a largely Scottish crew, including a bonnie highland laddie, a maid of Isla, the lovely lass of Inverness, the sweetest lad called Jamie, and the one who was the lad of everyone's heart, Willy. Beethoven got a little heavier with *The Massacre of Glencoe* and *The Return of Ulster*, and overall it was an admirable Gaelic output.

Primarily, it was for Edinburgh publisher George Thomson, who as secretary of the Board for the Encouragement of Arts and Manufactures in Scotland, kept a keen lookout for new talent. Thomson kept sending folk songs for Ludwig to "arrange" for voice, cello, piano and violin, and add instrumental intros and postludes to, and the composer kept obliging, doing nearly 200 such derangements before becoming deranged. Still, he was close to broke if not Baroque, and it paid the bills. He also wanted an in to that English-speaking society, and one way to get there was with Celtic folksong.

Joseph Haydn also jumped on the Celtic folksong bandwagon, with any number of arrangements for composted Celtacholic songs (often ballads by Sir Walter Scott and Scotch-loving Robert Burns), including the Welsh song *Ash Grove*-cum all its other names. *Roslin Castle* and *The White Cockade* or *My Love Was Born in Aberdeen* also tickled his clavichord.

He composed the first set of 100 Celtic folk arrangements in 1791, and the result the following year saved a publisher called Napier from bankruptcy. Haydn also found he enjoyed slumming around in Celtic folksong, and did about 600 Irish, Scottish, Welsh and English pieces. He used plenty of "violin and basso continuo," pianoforte, keyboards and cello in doing it, but damn it, he was a Classic.

His star pupil, Ignaz Joseph Pleyel – who annoyed the master by playing rival concerts in London, and in fact looked like taking over from Haydn – also jumped on the European-adoption-of-Celtic-folksong movement. Pleyel provided George Thomson with six sonatas based on Scottish airs, and symphonies and accompaniments to 32 Scottish songs. He got over £130 for this lot (not bad in 1793), though his relationship with the editor was marred by the latter's view of such composers as "eccentric" and unbusinesslike.

Certainly, Robert Burns seems to have held these "foreign composers" in suspicion, and wrote to the editor *"not to let Mr. Pleyel alter one iota or accent of these airs,"* Scottish music might seem wild and eccentric to Continentals, Burns spat, but let these songs' native features be preserved! As it turned out, Thomson fancied himself a poet and musician as well, and there was a lot of bickerring back and forth between himself and Burns while the printing presses clanked away.

Béla Bartók and Zoltán Kodály of the early 1900s didn't consciously go Celtic, but they have to be mentioned here. They teamed up to salvage the Hungarian goat-headed bagpipe from its stubborn demise in a land that had at least once been home to the Celts.

Kodály even tried to mimic the sounds of bagpipes and hurdy-gurdy when he couldn't find the real thing, played around with the idea of melody-only music, threw in an occasional pentatonic scale – big in Irish and other ancient cultures – and also wrote about the idea of song based on language rhythms that can't be written down, which is what your Scottish *canntaireachd* is all about.

Meanwhile, in Brittany, Guy Ropartz (1864-1955) really went to sea writing music for a staged novel *Iceland Fisherman*, then a romantic opera, *Le Pays* (The Country), about an Armorican anti-hero. Those who have listened to Ropartz's misty tone poem work claim to hear Wagner, Strauss, Elgar, and Erich Korngold, a German composer who leapt all over Hollywood with a musical sword for Errol Flynn movies.

Ropartz did plenty of highfalutin symphonies, motets, masses and psalms, but also Breton folksong in Dorian mode. In fact, he so ardently churned up the soil of his beloved homeland you'd have had to wear boots around him.

Galician composer Andres Gaos (1874-1959) headed for the hills with his *Symphony No. 2, En Las Montanas De Galicia,* before heading off to Argentina to join a mass of fellow emigrants. Anton Garcia Abril, born in 1933, simply got immersed in the music he did for *Divinas Palabras,* a Galician tragicomedy opera performed with the likes of Placido Domingo. There's a huge shepherd with fiery beard and a sacrificial ox, a clairvoyant bird (very Celtic), and goblins, witches, incest, dancing girls, deformity, nakedness, lust, alcoholism and death in reassuring quantity. Abril also had wind, rain and the sea to score for.

Irish composer Shaun Davey got even wetter, picking up where St. Brendan the Navigator and his 20th-century reincarnation, Atlantic adventurer Tim Severin, left off, and produced *The Brendan Voyage* (1980), an entire symphony for orchestra, but really written for the uillean pipes, played by master Liam O'Flynn. It thematically sails and plunges, sinks and soars, all the way from Ireland to Labrador.

Another composer who made waves was Scott Macmillan of Nova Scotia, Canada, who blessed us with *Celtic Mass for the Sea* (1993). Macmillan, who's fabled around with Canadian folklorist Helen Creighton, wrote this tour de force for mixed choir, Celtic ensemble and string orchestra/quartet from collections like the *Carmina Gadelica.*

Ottawa, Canada, composer Patrick Cardy stuck his oar into the Celtic waters with *Fhir a Bhata* (A Boatman), also taking time out from Glory Hallelujahs and French ensemble-stuff to do some *Dreams of the Sidhe* (all about Beltane and the Tuatha de Danaan), *Jig* and *Avalon.*

And now, a few modern hybriefs in the Celtic-classic arena:

The South Carolina Philharmonic Orchestra and Florida Celt-rock band Seven Nations – the Led Zeppelin of bagpipes – came together in a symphonic terror-deforce.

Climbing out of his *Liverpool Oratorio,* popfather Sir Paul McCartney shapeshifted a Celtic poem he'd written into 75-minute concert work, *Standing Stone.*

And Irish composer Bill Whelan's *Seville Suite* orchestral portrayal of Red Hugh O'Donnell and his 1601 flight to Spain, had enough multiCeltural pipes in it to totally folk everything up.

*

# Chapter 16

# Celtic Night at the Movies

Go aboard *Titanic* and you come away with the memory of music to sink ships. The soundtrack for this 1997 movie makes waves long after hull has vanished beneath Atlantic. But studios have been giving us some really sound tracks and takes on the Celtic experience for decades, and it's not over yet.

The Highlands and Islands of Scotland have been musically evident for some time, and subtlety is not exactly the point in 1936 classic *Mary of Scotland*, starring Katharine Hepburn as the harried Queen of Scots. Sixteenth-century pipe-bands-with-torches come blaring and thundering down the road whenever anyone makes a statement.

Things are more understated in the 1971 version of *Mary, Queen of Scots,* with Vanessa Redgrave as the red-haired royal who acts and reacts to composer John Barry's music. Barry scored previous historical love-hate fests like *Anne of the Thousand Days* (1970) and *The Lion In Winter* (1968), and *Mary* is full of nice pizzicato woodwinds, weeping harps and violins. It's full of action, too, and a lot of trumpet-timpani-strings-and-horn suggest Barry's other action flicks like *You Only Live Twice, On His Majesty's Secret Service* and *Thunderball.*

For some light relief, there's the Broadway play that became the 1954 film *Brigadoon,* in which two idlers find themselves in a Scottish kingdom too good to be true. This Lerner and Loewe lightweight stars endless bagpipes, songs like *Once in the Highlands, Heather on the Hill* and *Almost Like Being in Love.* Cyd Charisse is ravishing, but the ensemble choruses are more Broadway than bracken, while Gene Kelly is too buttoned-down to be a real Celt, but wows them in any era with those dancing vocals.

*Whiskey Galore* (1948) is a merry musical romp that achieves closure to all those laments for whiskey. In this film, whiskey is not "banned," it's just not to be plentifully found in the village until a shipwreck proves once again that long-running magic of Celtic waters. Islanders spirit kegs of the stuff away from navy officers, and there's a lot of those old Celtic "strains" of happy music and lullaby stuff, as jubilant pubgoers dance up a storm, hide bottles in babies' cradles, and more.

Things get heavier in two 1995 films. *Rob Roy* pitted Liam Neeson against nasty 18th century landowners and a Carter Burwell score, with tracks like *Dispossessed* and *Procession for the Ill-Used.* Scottish folk-rock group Capercaillie, and musicians who would go on to appear in *Riverdance*, also contribute some heart-Robbing stuff.

A woad-painted Mel Gibson came charging on the screen as 14th-century hero William Wallace in *Braveheart.* Scottish Highland and Irish uillean pipes mix for maximum effect and confusion in this James Horner-scored epic. It's full of numbers like *Betrayal and Desolation, After The Beheading* and *You Have Bled With Wallace* that are bloody good. In fact, it's enough to make you forget about the 1986 film *Highlander,* even if that one was about a time-traveller who just wouldn't die.

Wales gets some nice airplay with oldies *How Green Was My Valley* and *The Stars Look Down,* both about the troubles and triumphs of coal miners. *Green,* a John Ford-directed vehicle with a starry cast, beat *Citizen Kane* for Best Film in 1941, and musicmeister Alfred Newman is in there somewhere. His orchestrated folksy soundtrack includes *Huw Walks Among the Daffodils, Mother* and *Huw in Broken Ice*, *Huw's Lesson*, and *Huw Finds His Father*, and a Welsh choir give it all they've got, to make you forget this Welsh village was constructed entirely on a set in Malibu, California.

*The Quiet Man* (1952) did go on location, which was Ireland, and John Wayne and Maureen O'Hara caper through musical numbers like *I'll Take You Home Again Kathleen*, *St. Patrick's Day*, *Mary Kate* and *My Mother* and stop off in Innisfree, Castle Town and Humble Cottage. This movie has done more to create an Irish image for millions of Americans than almost any other film.

For others, it's *Ryan's Daughter*, which lushes up love and hate in the 1916 Irish Rebellion. The Seven Years War wends its way into *Barry Lyndon* (1975), but so does folk group The Chieftains, pioneers at bringing trad instruments into films. Songs like *Women of Ireland* and *Piper's Maggot Jig* blend surprisingly well with the soundtrack's cello concertos, German dances, sarabandes for duels, and trio Handel-Mozart-and-Schubert. This folk-meets-classical approach was a natural for this 18th-century arms-and-amour offering.

In *Patriot Games* (1992), pipes and drums propel Harrison Ford and Anne Archer into the midst of Irish terrorism, with numbers like *Attack on the Royals* and *Highland Execution*, while otherworldly female voices haunt slower moments. Some feel *Patriot* composer James Horner used some of his thematic material from *Aliens,* but as fear is a great factor in both films, most listeners forgave him. *In The Name of the Father, Some Mother's Son, Michael Collins* and *Veronica Guerin* also gave us troubled times with memorable music, and especially memorable is Irish rock group U2's anthem for *Father.*

However, the struggles arguably are easier for five sisters surviving on a 1930s farm in *Dancing at Lughnasa* (1998). In the film, pagan festivals still beckon the churchgoing, with harvest fires lit to Lugh the Sun God.

Composer Bill Whelan, who had been Riverdancing for a few years, gives us plenty of emotion, aided by trad musicians, a few sprightly reels, and Irish balladeer Dolores Keane singing Yeats's poem *Down By The Salley Gardens.* "Salley," by the way, is a kind of tree, and by now we know the arboreal passions of the Celts. *Dancing At Lughnasa* also has danced its way into countless community theatres.

*Angela's Ashes,* a book-cum-film about being dirt poor in Limerick, reaches a low drone indeed, and there's no music dreary enough for the young narrator's laments about being forced to take Irish dancing lessons. However, John Williams' music, like *Lord, Why Do You Want the Wee Children?* and *If I Were In America*, is jazzed up with pieces like *The Dipsy-Doodle* and *Pennies From Heaven.* After all, this was ragtime time, and even the Irish got it.

They also got it in *Titanic*, which scooped the 1997 Academy Award for best dramatic score and was the first soundtrack to reach the Billboard chart's #1 slot. Here, chamber-ragtime is mixed with London Symphony Orchestra, synthesizer, and uillean pipes. Gaelic Storm, a Celtic band plucked out of a present-day California pub, kick up the rollicking rhythms of *John Ryan's Polka* and *The Blarney Pilgrim* as the steerage band for *Irish Party in Third Class.* Above-deck, Canadian diva Celine Dion belts out that things will go on, but the end comes with too soon, with a watery *Hymn To the Sea.*

The film *Songcatcher* crosses the ocean in a happier mood. A sisterly followup to 2000's roots-choked flick *O Brother, Where Art Thou?*, it brings a young English teacher (Janet McTeer) to the Appalachian hills as a "song-catcher" of old Scotch-Irish music. Between bad-mouthing from locals and getting plucked at by bearded banjo-picker Aidan Quinn, she's seduced with time-honoured pieces like *Wayfarin' Stranger, Moonshiner, Mary of the Wild Moor* and *The Cuckoo Bird,* performed by songbirds like Dolly Parton, Emmylou Harris and Roseanne Cash.

Banjo, harmonium, mandolin, mountain dulcimer, fiddle and more drone the message home that Celtic-cum-country is alive but sometimes ill. *Sounds of Loneliness* and *All My Tears* are gloomy, but *Wind and Rain* is gut-wrenching, because it's all about a fiddle made from the bones of a corpse. You'll find this kind of instrumental industry throughout Celtic history, and it was known as resourcefulness.

Lovestruck duo Tom Cruise and Nicole Kidman are resourceful enough to go *Far and Away* (1992) from Ireland to Oklahoma, accompanied now and then by The Chieftains, who play their way through *The Fighting Donnellys*, *Fighting For Dough*, and *End Credits*. Overall, the John Williams score brings together old and new lands in a folky orchestral wave of oceanic depth.

The Atlantic is no barrier for the Irish boy who goes time-travelling with a couple of magic imps in *Our Country* (2003). He gets nothing less than the whole story of the growth of country music from its Celtic roots to the Appalachian mountains, bluegrass, western swing, The Grand Ole Opry and brand new country, jazz and rock 'n' roll. Top tutors like Jimmie Rodgers, Dolly Parton, Loretta Lynn, Charlie Daniels, Porter Waggoner, Dwight Yoakam and The Dixie Chicks, sing the lad along on his journey, while film company IMAX gives us panoramic treatment of everything.

For old-town Celtic country Canadiana, it's tough to beat Sullivan Entertainment's offerings. Its films and TV programs like *Road to Avonlea, Wind at my Back* and *Love on the Land,* are full of musical tracks like *Celtic Prologue, Irish Mischief, Scottish Ode, The Molly Maguires* and *Women of Ireland.* In Sullivan productions, many a heart remains in the Highlands, and it's all infused with *Medley of the Celtic Mists.*

There's plenty of mist everywhere in *The Secret Of Roan Inish* (1995), an Irish delight about selkies – seal people – and real people, sealed by composer Mason Daring in a nicely eerie way. Ethereal female singing and gentle woodwinds permeate a track full of numbers like *Selkie Song* and *Piper's Lullaby*. Amongst the many musical contributors are Maire Breatnach and Ronan Browne, who would go swimming instrumentally right into early versions of the stage production *Riverdance*.

Canadian filmmaker John Walker's documentary *The Fairy Faith* (2000) crosses the water to look at fey folk from Skye to Nova Scotia, stopping at mystical rivers and pools along the way. Neo-ClassiCelt composer Scott Macmillan and band MacCrimmon's Revenge are gently instrumental in making you want to respect the fairies, even if you never see one. And such magic and mayhem brings us to:

## ARTHUR DOES L.A.

Some sketchy references before 1000 CE tell us that King Arthur was a Romano-Celtic chieftain and leader (probably from Wales), who rallied his Britons to hold back the encroaching Saxon barbarians in the fifth or sixth century.

Imaginative scribes in France, England, and Wales from the 12th century on, kitted Arthur out with a kingly and cuckolded status, a queen Guinevere, a cuckolder named Lancelot, a bratty son-of-a-nephew Mordred, magician Merlin, and enchantress Morgan Le Fay – a pretty reincarnation of the deadly Celtic *Morrigan* – all around a castle called Camelot that got bigger and more elaborate every year. By the Victorian age there were enough armored stars and weird goings-on to make Arthur an epic that just had to be staged.

None did it with more delight than the Broadway team of Allan Jay Lerner and Frederick Loewe. In their musical *Camelot,* which opened at Broadway's Majestic

Theater in 1960, they immersed us in *The Lusty Month of May*, told us *How to Handle A Woman*, cried out *Fie on Goodness!* and left us with the eternal question of *I Wonder What The King Is Doing Tonight?*

Lerner and Loewe musically embraced T.H. White's *The Once and Future King,* a book that treats a pseudo-medieval utopia with enough laughs to guarantee ovations. Presenting Richard Burton in green tights didn't hurt the effort, nor did Julie Andrews' crystalline capacity for Queen Guinevere and Robert Goulet's spearing of the Lancelot role. Bob did the knightly run very well, but aspired to greater things sometime after he began to roll out *If Ever I Would Leave You*, and by the 1970s was playing Arthur in remakes.

The 1967 film *Camelot* danced a lot with Richard Harris as Arthur-the-second and Vanessa Redgrave as a playful Guinevere. The movie was made when archeologists were digging around in Somerset, England for true Arthurian evidence, so it's no wonder Hollywood composer Alfred Newman had a field day adapting Loewe's masterpiece of a score for the big screen soundtrack, and that interactions got quite earthy between leading lovers. The 1968 hit single *MacArthur Park* became a lateral success for the ennobled Harris.

Before, during and after *Camelot,* there's much Arthuriana of note. Time-traveller Bing Crosby was the *Connecticut Yankee in King Arthur's Court* (1949) who loosened up royal musicmakers with some jazz and pizzazz, while *Monty Python and the Holy Grail* (1975) was a modal orchestral hoot with a couple of percussive coconuts for the road. With *Excalibur* (1981) Arthur and Co. rode again, in a grandiose, gruesome, and at times musically overbearing epic that owes something to Wagner, including the German heavy's *Funeral March to the Gods.* As Wagner was a descendent of the Saxons who annihilated Arthur and Co.'s Celts in the end, perhaps it's fitting he thunders all over this picture.

In 1995's *First Knight,* composer Jerry Goldsmith gave us authentic-sounding fifths for *Arthur's Fanfare* and the like; orchestral, choral, and plenty of percussion for action scenes, pomp and pageantry, and a *Lancelot's Theme* segment that's been likened to Mahler's *Second.* Goldsmith worked under late master Miklos Rozsa, who was chivalry personified in his 1950s scores for *Ivanhoe* and *Knights of the Round Table,* a sumptuous Arthurian offering.

Through *The Mists of Avalon* (TV, 2001) we get a welcome perspective through Arthurian females-of-note Igraine, Morgaine, Vivienne and Guinevere, with a bucolic soundtrack full of harps, strings and woodwinds. Whoopi Goldberg as professor Vivien Morgan becomes *A Knight in Camelot* (1998), through a computer malfunction. She mugs and miracle-works her way through the royal landscape to composer Patrick Williams' courtly efforts, which occasionally give way to The Four Tops' *Reach Out* (*I'll Be There*).

Time-travel effort *A Kid In King Arthur's Court* has a Disney feel-good score and nice stringwork by guitar's First Lady, Liona Boyd, but for animated Arthurian offerings, it's tough to beat Disney's 1998 *Quest for Camelot.* We get a dragon who sings like Elvis, and musical number *Looking Through Your Eyes* performed three times, by country singer LeAnne Rimes, Irish group The Corrs, and David Foster. Gary Oldman, Don Rickles, and Steve Perry of American rock group Journey, give us some adult-contemporary, a surprisingly subdued Celine Dion sings *The Prayer,* and opera singer Andrea Bocelli seconds this notion but with less restraint.

Two Thousand and four brought us a blockbuster simply called *King Arthur.* Hans Zimmer, who scored immensely with *Gladiator* and *Last Samurai,* uses plenty of electronic wizardry to orchestrate epic emotion for this armoured spectacle. King Arthur's getting older by the decade, and even the famous need a boost.

\*

# Chapter 17

# Rock 'n' Reel — In the Homelands

Try musically charting Ireland, Scotland and other Celtic lands, and you'll find myriad performers who leave you in no doubt as to their inclinations.

There's Celtic Cross, Ossian, Tuatha de Danann, Danu, Iona, Keltica, Blood Or Whiskey, Ceilidh Minogue, Blazin Fiddles, Peatbog Faeries, Ceolbeag, Clan Alba, Skara Brae, The Tartan Amoebas, Dordan (Irish for "drone"), and those just out to scare you – Hamish Mc-Doodle and the Kicking Keltic Kaos Krew, Wild Welsh Women, Band From County Hell, and The Sex Slaves From Hell.

Just understand that this is a modern phenomenon. Up to the 1960s, traditional music was an obscure thing, droning away around fens and hearth-fires, and all without any clever names. *Fleadh* and *feisanna* musical get-togethers had no real PR, while limelighters like Andy Stewart and Kenneth McKellar brogued parlor-and-stage music, "ceili bands" went for pianos and snare drums, and Irish dancers clattered their stiff-spined way along the competitive route to obscurity with recorded acordion music.

In the 1960s, John Reidy, a trained composer with enough Irish sensibilities to become Sean O'Riada, began bringing trad music and instruments like the bodhran into orchestras, radio, theaters, films and churches. He also tried to interest Benedictine monks in the connection between *sean-nos* and plainchant, to the extent of composing massive masses in Irish.

O'Riada formed Ceoltoiri Chualann, a group so good at being authentic they reformed as The Chieftains. With the uillean pipes, leadman Paddy Moloney began to blow away perceptions of those who thought bagpipes had to be big and mouthy. The Chieftains also went sailing over to Brittany and Galicia to trade rhythms.

In Ireland, they were challenged chiefly by four backstreet boys called The Dubliners, whose bushy beards rivaled their gritty traditional singing and playing, and who rival later American rockers ZZ Top as hair apparents. The tough quartet did a version of *Seven Drunken Nights*, learned from a *sean-nos* singer, and which bubbled up into the British charts. This liquified success was followed with *Whiskey on a Sunday*, *Seven Deadly Sins*, *More of the Hard Stuff*, and a beefed-up hymn called *Lord of the Dance*.

Their peers The Clancy Brothers were equally Irish, but with a more scrubbed appearance. This fraternal unit, who became as famous for their white Aran pullovers as their patriot songs, sang throughout Ireland and all the way across the Atlantic to become Tipperary Yanks, fuelled by their new persona of "folk musicians." Along the way, Clancy addition Tommy Makem picked up the modest titles of Bard of Armagh and Godfather of Irish Music.

But oh, the times were changing yet again by the early 1970s. Horslips, a spaced-out group of young neo-Fionnians, dressed up Celtic mythology on stage with lots of effects for spaced-out audiences. These advertising-industry guys knew how to package, even if their name itself was a fluke, the result of someone mumbling "Four Horsemen of the Apocalypse..." and "Four Poxmen of the Horslypse..." before coming up short.

The band maxed out mythsters like Chu Chulainn and the Morrigan, and singles like *King of the Fairies* and *Dearg Doom* flew up the charts. Horslips had became Celt-rockers ahead of their time, though, and ultimately their wings fluttered and folded and they crashed to earth, though not before prodding the dulled Irish-sensibilities of youngsters who wanted nothing to do with the Clancy Brothers or Sean O'Riada, but who might well go off and pull out their parents' records in the end.

Another band twisting up the trad was Thin Lizzy, who boasted the musical world's first black Celt headliner in leadman Phil Lynott. Phil and the boys hit it big when they took that old tune *Whiskey In the Jar* and rocked it out. This modernized paean to *uisge beatha*, the "water of life," shook up a lot of people, and it shook up Thin Lizzy enough to go back to their more modern macho stuff, but the die had been cast.

It heated up again with groups like De Danann (named after those legendary *Tuatha De Danaan*), Sweeney's Men, Planxty, Moving Hearts, and Patrick Street, infectious rock and reel with new trad instruments like the Celtic bouzouki and, occasionally, off-beat Eastern European timings like 9/16. These Foreign Service offerings were beefed up even more by De-Danann, who threw klezmer, black gospel and the Beatles into their brew.

The Afro-Celt Sound System gave us an Ireland-meets-West Africa mix, while the veins of Salsa Celtica flowed equally with liquid chili and Scotch. Other Scots stayed closer to home. Fiddler Aly Bain continually took a bow to the Shetland Islands, going afield to join Scottish/Irish mix Boys of the Lough. One James Miller entered the Gaelic arena as "Ewan MacColl," all the better to preserve traditional legacies and record "in the field." Agricultural interest also produced group Runrig, named after an old rural "land-use" pattern, and The Bothy Band.

Silly Wizard, which many people thought referred to Merlin in his later years, showed their true inclinations with LPs like *Caledonia's Hardy Sons,* though *So Many Partings* would herald their Highland clearance to America. If anyone can get the exiles back, though, it's fleeting "Wizard" member Dougie Maclean, who went solo to write song-cum-anthem *Caledonia.*

Meanwhile, The Battlefield Band put up their dukes with electric keyboards and the like, claiming *It Was All For Our Rightful King,* before taking off to some geographical anomaly called *Deserts of Tulloch,* pausing to let bagpipe player Mike Katz enter the Dubliners/ZZ Top Bearded Hall of Fame.

The punk Hall of Infamy produced groups stamped with warning labels, but Pogue Mahone simply invited people to "kiss my ass," which was what their name meant in Gaelic. Even after they shortened it to The Pogues, they remained the bad boys, with LPs like *Rum, Sodomy and the Lash.* They mixed originals like *Boys from the County Hell* with *The Bold Fenian Men* and *Poor Paddy,* going *Across The Broad Atlantic,* though a rough ocean voyage resulted in *Sickbed of Chu Chulainn.* The Pogues teamed up with The Dubliners to record old standard *The Irish Rover,* which bearded doubters with an in-your-face chart topper.

Irish angstress Sinead O'Connor faced off with shaved head and Papal picture ripoffs, but remained tied enough to the past to do songs like *I Am Stretched On Your Grave,* whose lyrics by Irish poet Frank O'Connor translate as a 12th-century Irish poem, *Ta me sinte ar do thuama.* It's a song in the style of that traditionally solo *sean-nos* singing.

Likewise, Van Morrison, who came out of Belfast band Them in the 1960s, off-and-soloed in the Celtic arena, further coloring his new *Brown-Eyed Girl* and *Blue Money* movement with 1973's *Purple Heather,* reviving a song the Clancy Brothers had as *Will You Go, Lassie, Go?*

145

With the help of master uillean pipers and the like, Van then began to growl out *One Irish Rover, Connswater* and *Celtic Swing, Irish Heartbeat* (both a song and an album with The Chieftains), *The Star of the County Down, My Lagan Love*, and *Celtic Ray*, an enlightened Morrison original. A more obscure recording revealed him doing poetic battle with ancient Irish hero Chu Chulainn.

Folk-rock bands Fairport Convention and Steeleye Span stirred up magic with time-traveller *Tam Lin*, and Tam's 13th-century cousin *Thomas the Rhymer*. The phenomenon of bands with otherworldly female lead singers continued with Clannad and its ethereal folk-rock. This Donegal clan gave us Irish Gaelic – along with bongos, synthesizers and voice overdubbing – as they rose from the mists to buy out much of the smoke-machine industry. Little sister Aithne eventually fought her way out of the fog to become one of the biggest Irish-export industries ever as Enya.

She also became the gauge by which others were measured. One "new Enya" was Karen Matheson of Capercaillie, a winsome foursome that cornered the TV market, with sounds for *A Prince Among Islanders* and *Highlanders*, and reminded us that *The Blood is Strong*. Mairead Ni Mhaonaigh dove into Altan, both the name of a mystical Irish pool and a band full of *Blackwater, Roaring Water* and *Over The Water to Bessie*. Aquatic gave way to the anthropomorphic, in their songs like *Uncle Rat, Horse With a Heart* and lesser contender *Red Crow*.

As the Celts revered the furred-and-feathered crowd, it's not surprising there's been a certain amount of animal magnetism in the movement, with The Bumblebees, DeffGoat, Four Men and a Dog, and Old Blind Dogs (the last two, cousins of Dutch group Hair of the Dog), The Wolfe Tones and to watch over it all with dubious efficiency, Deaf Shepherd.

Things got deafer yet with the psychofolkadelia acid-croft sounds of bands like Shooglenifty, who threw in distortions, rave rhythms, synthesizers, sonic mutations, and juxtapositions galore, to periodically go travelling beyond their homeland and homage to *Maggie Ann of Clachnabrochen*, with *Bjork's Chauffeur, The Hijab* and *Schuman's Leap*.

Welsh group Ar Log showed some smarts in their very name, which means "for hire." Sian James began to harp under a "Welsh Enya" label but doing well on her own, Llio Rhydderch carried on the unbroken *tinc* genealogy of the ancient harpers, and musicologist-crusader Robin Huw Bowen became lord of the Welsh triple-harp. Bob Delyn a'r Ebillion have funked up folk, and bands like Llwyrbr Llaethog, Datblygu and Gorky's Zygotic Mynci provide more linguistic workouts. The *pibgorn* and *pibacwd* have continued to drone out regional preferences in Wales, and it looks like they're here to stay.

In Cornwall, Merv Davey and *troyl* band Pyba have donned costume and regional instruments to keep history alive. In fact, Davey became honorary piper of the Cornish *gorsedd* bardic arena, and that's practically royalty. Cornish group Bucca gave us a wide-open look at Cornish tradition with *The Hole in the Harper's Head*, while family group Anao Atao revealed that the bombarded link with Brittany was alive and well, and ready to throw some *Esoteric Stones*.

Charles Guard is a solo harper who's pretty well become the king of modern Manx music, and his administratorship of The Manx Heritage Foundation indicates a ruler who knows his history. The Tholtan Builders went for the foundations of tholtans, the deserted homesteads of immigrant hill farmers. The most famous Manx group ever, the Bee Gees, put aside their Australian-American re-invention long enough to bring old Manx folksong *Ellan Vannin* to the previously unaware.

London, as well as England improper, has plenty of Eire-apparent bands, and easterly-inclined musicians who have mixed Muslim vocals and classical Indian lyric-and-melody specialties with the key ornaments of British folk tradition. Other Gaels have joined Continentals to find multiCeltural common chords, and vice versa.

Many neo-Celts in the Highlands and islands simply looked west for musical inspiration.

The Barry McCabe Band infused Irish with blues, while Edinburgh group Swamp Trash presented psycho-bluegrass. More traditional bluegrass and jugband string bands began to ferment, especially in the bottlenecks of Cork, Ireland.

If you're still with me at this point, just rest asunder that there are any number of other Celtic stars rocking, folking, funking and fugueing, keeping alive bombarded history, blindsided bards, and any number of Celtic subjects and predilections.

## CONTINENTAL DRIFT AND DRONE

One of the biggest Breton names still is Alan Stivell, who founded the Celtic Harp New Age in the early 1970s. Alan, whose original surname was "Cochevelou,"wanted something snappier, though would have to add "father of contemporary Breton folk revival." But though he sang and played Z lore to the max, he also began to pick up the discordant rhythms of the Far East, American natives and black spirituals, pleased to find a common meeting ground.

Groups like Tri Yann also were big on reviving traditional Breton music, but not too separatist to include influences like Irish and American. Brittany's Z language is well represented with Pozaout (Breton for "cowboy"), rock band Kroazhent, dance band Skeduz, and jazzy ballad band Gwerz. But by the letter, Barzaz have them beat with their takes on Hersart de Villemarque's *Barzaz*

*Breizh* 19th-century song collection, while lesser-known group ZZZ do primarily lullabies.

Asturian band Felpeyu got alphabetically fixated with musical offerings like rhythms of *munieras, muneres,* and *mulineiras,* as well as X-rated, with song *Xirandlyes,* one band member named Xuan and several from the town of Xixon. Another grouping, Llan de Cubel, maxed out the C word in LPs full of *Interceltique, Celtica* and *Celtas.*

In Galicia you'll find musicians who think 13th-century Martin Codax's *Cantigas de Amigo* and *Amor* are worth doing a song and dance about. You'll also get bombarded by the bombarde, and blown away by the Galician bagpipes. *Gaita* godfather Carlos Nunez is a dynamo who's also blown himself right into dueling-chanter recordings with The Chieftains. Bagpipe babe Susana Seivane has done for Galician folk music what Ofra Harnoy and Lara St. John have done for classical, while massed females like As Pandereteiras de Cantigas e Agarimos and Faltriqueira carry on the tradition of *pandeireteras,* gaily dressed women who run with the tambourines and sing their guts out in Gallego.

Os Cempes (The Centipedes) team Galician pipes with Galician whistle, and accordion, cowbell and claves. You'd think Galician band Milladoiro, with a name that means "heaps of stones gathered by shepherds," is equally folkified, but they've been known to launch themselves right into the orchestral arena, with lofty projects like *Iacobus Magnus* (The Great Jacob), that Santiago de Compostela apostle of the tourism industry.

The band Durindaina scoured the same area for old bagpipe tunes and took the path of least electronic resistance, with instruments like shell drums. Leixapren dedicated album *Gaitropos* to a devilish creature who's half-man, half-bagpipe, possibly a comment on the many piping band members. Trisquel took themselves and their

*Cantigas de Amigo* along a path with instruments like the hurdy-gurdy-ish *zanfona,* and band Laio took their gaita-and-bass-clarinet couplings right into the modern club scene.

Slavic band Carrantuohill would rather just take the path to the top, and that's what their name means. On the *Rocky Road to Dublin* and infused with the *Magic of Celtic Rings,* they liven up Polish versions of Woodstock, and have flocked with Deaf Shepherd and deafened crowds with The Battlefield Band. *The Speed Celts,* one of Carrantuohill's greatest hits, have a distant cousin in band The Orthodox Celts from Belgrade, Serbia.

If Slainte and Six Steps to the Bar are music for many throats, Celtic teetotalers welcome Sweden's effervescent Mountain Dew. Those who like their plaid doubled may go for Clonakilty, while others *Get Reel* with Belgian band Urban Trad, and travel Italian musical roads with band Tuatha De Dannan, and Hungarian roots with Dagda.

Eureka, Jacky Tar, and Claddagh have done some funkin' Celticisms in Australia and New Zealand, while down-under band Cotter's Bequest got earthy with Welsh, Manx and Cornish music, just to prove they're in no Desert of Tulloch. Japan and Mexico have pipes and drums, Hong Kong has the Gaelic Gaul to contribute, and Israel's Yarok Ad, or Evergreen, show that Irish and Hebrew can pine away with relative roots.

It goes on and on, but let's just close by saying that German group Drowning Bagpipes tend to feature every instrument but aerophones, so as the CD goes, they give many *A Reason to Live.*

*

# Chapter 18

# Rock 'n' Reel, New World —
# Celts are U.S!

Anyone who has the Gaul to question whether American musicians are having Gaels of fun with the whole thing, please take note:

There are bands like Celtic Dragon, Celtic Clan, Celtic Cross, Celtic Heart, Celtic Core, Celtic Nots, Celtic Confusion, SuperKeltic, Keltic Cross-Fire, Tartanic, and Three Men In Kilts. Cwn Annwn is the Ameri-Welsh no-vowel winner, while Irish Hearts is the result of *ceili*-meets-Hawaiian *luau.* You'll also find Brigid's Cross, Bad Haggis, The Young Dubliners, Highland Sun, Full Gael, Gaelic Tribe and The Suffering Gaels.

And if you remember the general regard in which Celts held trees, you'll appreciate Distant Oaks, Blackthorn, Blackwood, Mountain Laurel Ceili Band and Spooky Tree.

Other rad plaid bands go far with the comparison route, hence the "Chieftains on Caffeine" description of the jig-punk Prodigals. The liquidated-lament connection is evident in groups like 3 Pints Gone and Empty Flask, and the mystical, in Iona, Avalon Rising, Bedlam Bards, Broceliande and The Drivelling Druids.

Aisling ("Ashling") is a band that gets reel with musical visions, just as the Aisling dream-vision in Irish mythology often represented the homeland. "Seven Nations" refers to those seven Celtic nations, and California band The Whooligans pay tribute to Irish oldtimers like The Clancys and

The Dubliners, but seem also to have been influenced by Irish terrors The Pogues, and end up by saying their style is nobody's fault but their own.

As the Irish seem to have had a lot to do with settling America, it's not surprising a group of Irishmen got the whole modern American Celtic music scene going. Family-and-friend unit The Clancy Brothers and Tommy Makem got a warm welcome with their slew of fightin' feelin' songs and sagas, in the 1950s and '60s New York coffeehouses as well as at Carnegie Hall. An 18-minute appearance on *The Ed Sullivan Show* turned them into a big folk group, but it didn't turn their heads. The Clancy crew wore their hearts on their sleeves.

In fact, a bloody pullover decorated their early LP *The Rising of the Moon,* the name of a Celtacholic song about the Irish uprising of 1798. The Clancys also had taken Dominic Behan's song *The Patriot Game* into the folk clubs, and a newcomer called Bob Dylan (who began as a Zimmerman) translated it as *God On Our Side.*

The tune actually had come from the Appalachians as *The Merry Month of May*, and become popularized as *Bold Grenadier* by 1940s big ballad singer Jo Stafford. Or so some say. It was the same kind of multi-personality stuff that had surrounded traditional songs for centuries, and radio programs like *Echoes of Erin* and *Tangled Tuatha Tales* perpetuated it.

This goldmine of tarted-up trad, with its themes of love, lust, war, mistaken identities and other biggies, was inhaled by a spaced-out crowd who liked the poignant stuff and were fine with the wars of a few hundred years ago, while that Vietnam business needed lots of music to get through. Folkie hotspots like New York's Greenwich Village dished up performers several generations removed from "Celtic," if at all connected. Desire overruled birth, and anyone with a guitar, a dulcimer or something weirder, was happy to jump on the Old World and groove it out

As time went on, a lot of them got downright weepy about a homeland they'd never seen. For throat-clogging emotion, you can't get thicker than modern Irish-American Peter Jones's song *Kilkelly*. This heartrending hello-goodbye series of fatherly letters-to-a-son-in America over a span of 32 years from 1860 on, takes almost that long to play and hear.

Bands like Off the Boat, Americay and The Emigrants are evidence America is not about to forget this chapter of history. Not only that, a lot of Americans would argue their own kind, through that Scots-Irish influx, has dragged on Celtic musical traditions longer than the homeland. As well, Irish beats mixed with African rhythms to become rock music. The bodhran backbeat of jigs and reels also morphed into the train-beat of rockabilly, and hence to rock 'n' roll.

That's the thinking of American longtime folk-rocker Henk Milne, known as the "big voice" of The Volunteers, a band equally inspired by the Volunteers who held Dublin against the British Army in 1916 and an LP by 1960s California acid-rockers Jefferson Airplane who held the age of psychedelia against the PTA.

This folk-rock progression is why Milne and his crew have happily embarked on what purists would scream sacrilege, writing lyrics to Turlough O'Carolan's 17th- and 18th-century tunes, and rocking them out. O'Carolan, it seems, was a bawdy old jokester who actually penned words to a lot of his tunes, so welcome to keeping tradition alive in the new land.

Milne's band Voluntarily takes time-honored Celtic themes into LPs like *Whiskey, Love and Disaster,* not a bad reference to Celtic history as a whole. They're also something of an anomaly in a south-Florida scene that's always gone for the Latin dance-flavored stuff, but as The Vols are called a full-throttle runaway locomotive of a band, that may have changed by now.

Equally in love with tradition, if less invasive, are Rhode Island's Aubrey Atwater and Elwood Donnelly. Among the many lyrical and percussive instruments they play are wooden puppets hit with a paddle to make them dance. In Ireland and America, "limberjacks" traditionally were made in the image of the maker. This opens up some interesting possibilities on the voodoo-doll idea, to which further research may find a Celtic connection. We can already figure out "paddy whack."

For Atwater-Donnelly, percussion also is a feat of feet; female half Aubrey Atwater (who hasn't let an early classical music education stop her) has mastered the feat of clogging and banjo-ing at the same time. A.D. do a lot of imaginative original stuff, but their version of *Kilkelly* is one of their most-requested pieces, and a lot of Celtacholia to keep living up to.

Ireland gets plenty of Eire-play through the U.S, but Virginia band Moch Pryderi went for Wales and Brittany, which often gets lost in the whole Celtic arena. The band's name is Welsh for "Pryderi's Pigs," and that all goes back to that Welsh poetic saga, *The Mabinogion*. Moch Pryderi's version tells us that the notable Pryderi, having lost his crashing boars to his nemeses, cast a spell on his death-bed that the pigs would wallow in dirt, and disgust everyone around them. Some of the pigs, though, were changed into musicians to provide music for the deserving.

M.P. have gone whole-hog with this, and are so glad to be "dancing in the pigsty" they named an album exactly that. They've also supplemented the Celtic "P" Brythonic language of Wales and Brittany with the Celtic "B" language, as their instruments include the bagpipes, bouzouki, biwbo, the Breton bombarde, the bodhran, and the pibgorn, that Welsh hornpipe that droned on long after the constantly-pickled poet Robert Burns lost the Scottish version.

Americans embrace the ins and outs of Celtic hystery, paying homage to old deities in reincarnations of obscure works like *The Wooing of Etain*. As Etain ruled sun, water, transmigration of souls and more, she's still good to have on your side. California band Distant Oaks milks the *Carmina Gadelica,* that sacred collection so lovingly put together by 19th-century Scottish composter Alexander Carmichael. Appropriately enough, this D.O. recording is rich with reel chants, songs, blessings and poems, and an impressive variety of strings, tones and drones.

The Scottish smallpipes, a more demure-than-the-Highland-version instrument, that considers itself a cross between clarinet and violin, drone on with band Iona Abbey, in Seattle, Washington. However, Iona also go for the Highlands in air play, and when the group's founding member began moonlighting as a Resident Cathedral Bagpiper, we could rejoice in further evidence that the patronage system was still alive and in Americay.

In certain instances, the bagpipes have been thoroughly re-invented. In name, there's Bad Haggis's "bagtar," which is what they call their dueling bagpipes-and-guitar. Colorado group Gobs O' Phun took a harmmonica and attached a balloon that plays a drone, their "Gobs O' Phun bagpipe." Phun's approach to the requisite Irish stuff is represented in *These Gobs Are Revolting: A Collection of Historical Rebel Tunes,* and *Liverdance: A Collection of Celtic Drinking Songs.*

*Uisge beatha* (Gaelic for "water of life" – i.e., whiskey) and other potables continue to inspire many musicians, though Chicago band Three Men In Kilts acknowledge with their CDs that *Thirsty Work It Is* and *It's Still Thirsty Work – Ten Years On!* Three Hams on Rye out of North Carolina are actually a pair, but like they say, if you're seeing only two of them you haven't had enough to drink. In that case, it's *Haste to the Whiskey, All For Me Grog,* and *Jackson's Bottle o'Brandied Keg.*

The "Hams" are not the only band with a missing musician. Kentucky group Rua (Gaelic colloquialism for "red") have let us know that at least one band member doesn't exist. Those 12-plus instruments? Handled by a synthesizer in a kilt. Rua once were known as that gargly Gaelic word for "whiskey," and apparently know something about shape-shifting.

California Celt-rockers The Fenians have soaked willing audiences with *Token Whiskey Song* and *Every Day's A Hooley.* That grand Irish pub song, though, gets subtitled *Tom Dooley Part 2,* a nice American touch lest anyone think this rowdy bunch figuratively is stuck in Ireland. *Rebel Sons of Erin* could do no better to reflect the band's name.

New York band Black 47 took that terrible year of 1847, the worst year of the Irish potato famine, and ran with it, throwing in some uillean piping, boombox beats, saxophone and African-Latin rhythmic drumming. Though they've rapped out some reggae, they've paid homage to Celtic history, all right, and get especially serious with songs like *I Got Laid on James Joyce's Grave* and *Bodhrans on the Brain,* while one member toned it down enough to create a *Keltic Kids* LP for the younger set.

Then Black 47's cop-cum-piper adopted the moniker Seanchai to perform *C'mon Ya Boyz in Green,* hooking up with a band called The Unity Squad, whose moods since then have gone from *Wanna Be Hip-Hop* to *Mise Eire.*

Some confusion arose when Scott M.X. Turner and The Devil's Advocates mixed Ireland's six-county fighting with Black civil rights stuff in three-song CD *The Battle of Aughrim.* Stores, it seemed, were stumped by just where to place a "punk/reggae/hiphop/trad Irish/techno" product. However, bands like The Lash, Flogging Molly, The Filthy Thieving Bastards and The Dropkick Murphys can be found under subsections of "tough."

Celtic worlds away from all that are mystical groups like Elvendrums, a Missouri mix who donned fanciful garb and pointed ears to claim kinship with the Tuatha de Danaan, the ancient Irish race descended from mother goddess Danu and ultimately forced underground to become fairies. The members of Avalon Rising visit Other-worlds, hobbit worlds, and the musical court of King Alfonso X, with themes of selkies, circle dances, God-the-female, and paying the piper – and have set a record for performing in other magically named bands like Bell-taine, Broceliande, Annwn and Magic Fire.

Broceliande (Bro-*say*-lee-ahnd), named after a Bret-on jungle where magician Merlin got bungled by the doubly enchanting Viviane/Nimue, have done a lot of things, like their Tolkien-themed LP *Starlit Jewel,* by hob-bit. So have The Brobdingnagian (*Brahb'ding-nag-ee-en*) Bards whose album *Memories of Middle Earth* has a "Tolkien" hit single amongst its 16 hobbitual songs that end with the *Psychopathic, Chronic, Schizophrenic Gollum Blues.*

There are no bigger Tolked-up fans than in the U.S., and author J.R.R. Tolkien's obsession with "Celtic" the-mes of crazy quests, noble leaders, bards, dragons, elves and elven affairs in general, apparently makes for irre-sistible song material today. You'll also find plenty of medieval music, while the long-running historical-re-enactment Society For Creative Anachronism has filled North America with as many bards as warriors.

There are plenty of Americans keeping alive the planxties, ports and pararhythms of old bards like O'Carolan, the two Rory Dalls and *mhor.* Neck and neck, country music continues to show its Celtic roots of misery and merriment. "New country" headliner Ricky Skaggs, who's played with The Chieftains, has put out a *Ceili Music* label, and many musicmakers are equally welcome at The Grand Ole Opry and any Celtic festival within bardic reach.

Groups like Four Shillings Short have given us musical multiculturalism with American Indian and East Indian rhythms. The classic example of all-female Ensemble Galilei came from several different states to graft Baroque on to Celtic, while two other women classically trained as they come, discovered going Gaelic with the guys in Constant Billy (named for an old British Morris dance reference) was a crack way to go.

Texas-based Constant Billy was wide open enough to mingle some European gypsy-jazzy Hot Club of Paris sounds with rock riffs a la The Ventures or Buddy Holly, and a fiddle that doowops as dizzily as it folks around. Still, the quartet has stopped off long enough for tradition in songs like *Rattlin' Roarin' Willie*, about the eternal fiddler's dilemma of having to decide between selling the fiddle and getting drinks, and keeping the instrument and going thirsty. By now, it should be quite obvious the Celts were an oral culture.

And few Celt-rock bands have proved to be mouthier than California bagrockers The Wicked Tinkers, with their Highland bagpipes, Celtic Bronze Age horn and Australian didgeridoo. The fact that the band's Wayne Belger has lung power to play a hollowed-out tree trunk would turn any old Celt green with envy, and it's the kind of thing that keeps the Ogham music industry alive.

Well, all of this suggests a lot of crack, as in *craic*, Gaelic for a certain spirit that "happens" or happens to be in the bottle. Shooting it up with sacred, medieval, funk and punk, world, jazz, hogs and hip-hop, bag-rock, shamrock 'n' roll, and bags of *mhor* is maybe only to be expected, considering how big this land is. It's enough to make you want to sing "AmeriCelt The Bountiful," and if so, that's all in keeping with reworking traditional songs to keep them alive.

*

## Chapter 19

# Rock 'n' Reel/ New World — Can-Celts

"Celts Are Us" is something Canada also feels strongly about.

This has to be obvious in bands with names like: Celtae, Celtic Attack, Celtic Clutter, Celtic Offspring, Celtic Eire, MacKeel (with album *Plaid*), Bourrasque Celtique, and Ceilidh Revue.

Then there's Skye Consort, Sons of Skye, The Tartan Terrors, Kilt, Scantily Plaid, Enter The Haggis, Sons of Gael, Oran, Out Of Alba, Banshee, Barley Brae, Taliesin, *Lochaber*, Hunting McLeod, MacCrimmon's Revenge, Crofter's Revenge, and Figgy Duff, named after a kind of Newfoundland-Irish party food.

It all just had to happen, and one motivational factor for it was an early-1970s CBC TV documentary called *The Vanishing Cape Breton Fiddler.* This Almost-Missing Persons bulletin galvanized a lot of Capers into action. The music actually was alive and well, droning out all over with masters like fiddler Winston "Scotty" Fitzgerald, and musical MacMasters, MacNeils, MacDonalds and MacCanadians galore. It just needed some young blood and good PR.

Cape Breton musicians like John Allan Cameron got that going. Donning a kilt for performances in big-city bars, he began bringing Scottish pipe music, on a 12-string guitar, to the world. He also dipped into the 3,000-fiddle tune repertoire of his uncle Dan Rory MacDonald. It helped take John Allan (who wowed audiences on TV and at The Grand Ole Opry) all the way to become Canada's Godfather of Celtic Music, joining Ireland's Tommy Makem in the Mario Puzo-and-*Mhor* Hall of Fame, about the same time Newfoundland's Minnie White became First Lady of the Accordion.

Lord of the Tears Canadian tenor John McDermott picked up the additional title of *Danny Boy,* his first LP before he went off to tour with The Irish Tenors as well as with himself. Some less defined lads became Buddy Wasisname and The Other Fellers, while other fellas became Men of the Deep, a Nova Scotian choir that mined the depths of Celtacholia, and occasionally teamed up with songbird Rita MacNeil. Nothing if not inspired, she's even gone down a mine shaft herself, grist for songs like *Workin' Man.*

Others like Newfoundland group The Irish Descendants showed the movement would live on and that in fact it would, as Rock band Great Big Sea label it, *Rant and Roar.*

Some bands would acknowledge The Irish Rovers and Ryan's Fancy, who took the Eire across the ocean to Canada in the 1960s and 70s. Fancy performed *The Rocky Road to Dublin* in an Arctic Bay igloo between numbers like *The Squid Jiggin' Ground* and *Green Shores of Fogo* (Newfoundland); the Rovers began serving audiences who didn't want "all 28 verses of *Mary Hamilton*" but were open to briefs on the whole thing.

Between horning in with songs like *Unicorn,* it's true the Rovers were responsible for a lot of Irish kitsch in Canada, reaching the apex of this climb up the shillelagh-of-stardom when they created costumed personas The Twerp, Bunworrier, and Willie the Leprechaun. Still, they roved all over to awaken dormant Celts, and to provide traditional music that didn't come with a 100-year-sleep tag.

However, that never disallowed lullabies, and that ancient music-strain of *suantraige.* After all, entire Cape

Breton families are known to make music right from the cradle. This clannish crooning scenario gave us The Rankins and The Barra MacNeils, Gaelic angels not averse to mixing trad with pop, jazz and punk. Two younger MacNeils teamed up with some pals to become *Slainte Mhath*. It's pronounced "Slawncha va," which means – and we're relieved to hear this – "Good Health to you." Their album titled *Va* gives neophytes the kind of phonetic help that should be more evident in the movement.

The clannishness continued with bouncy band Barachois (three siblings and a friend); the three Ennis Sisters, The Cottars' two pairs of brothers and sisters, and band Beolach, comprising run-off Rankins, MacNeils and MacIsaacs. Two of the most renowned families tied their bows in 2002, when fiddler Natalie MacMaster, niece of legendary Buddy MacMaster, wed fierce-fiddling frontman Donnell Leahy of Ontario octet Leahy. Long before this union, though, Natalie was kicking up her heels in the kind of simultaneous fiddling-step-dancing feat Cape Breton prides itself on, with a little Michael Jackson moonwalking for variety.

*The Vanishing Cape Breton Fiddler* did some extreme shapeshifting as the devil who came snarling out of the kitchen, with Natalie's cousin Ashley MacIsaac. Low-key LP titles like *Hi, How Are You Today?* notwithstanding, Ashley began to leap over bonfires, stages and audiences in army boots, neo-Celtic costumery, and sometimes half-naked. Crack attack was a mild term for what he did to the fiddle, and many traditionalists denounced him. His antics both on and off stage also resulted in the title of his autobiography, *Fiddling With Disaster*.

Classically trained violinist David Greenberg didn't fiddle with disaster at all, because his schooling notwithstanding, this American came to be regarded as one of the few "outsiders" to master Cape Breton music. He formed the group *Puirt a Baroque*, Scottish Gaelic for "mouth music," and the group's dual inclinations are evident in its recording *Bach Meets Cape Breton.*

Hip Cape Breton solo songstress Mary Jane Lamond simply sings in Gaelic, and though subtitles would be nice, you have to appreciate her single-mindedness. J.P. Cormier took a different route, all the way to Nashville to fiddle along with the likes of Waylon Jennings, Earl Scruggs and Travis Tritt. However, doing an LP called *Return to the Cape* was just too much for him, and it sent J.P. right out of The Grand Ol' Opry and home again to become a headliner who plays just about every string-ed instrument in existence.

Other headliners have inspired regional classics, like *Brenda Stubbert's Reel* and *Sandy MacIntyre's Trip To Boston.* In fact, fiddler Sandy, who got Steeped in Tradition with family members and friends, has been spotted playing and teaching all over North America.

The strung-out record probably has been set by Barrage, a Calgary, Alberta-based barrage of young fiddlers, under a dozen, but cloned to about 100 in sheer energy. They caper and cavort all over with their dueling bows, and their debut show *A Violin Sings, A Fiddle Dances,* gives us another good answer to that timeless question.

However, the fiddliest Canadian province has to be Prince Edward Island. Within this 140-mile strip of lobster-red soil, you'll find enough regionally distinctive styles, high-voltage attacks, bedevilled rhythms, snaps and cuts to make your head reel, if not your feet. Fiddlers like bow-shredding Richard Wood have pounded the island into the briny and well into world awareness.

Celtadian music-makers are good enough at what they do to go show the homelands a thing or two. This overseas-mission movement has included Cape Bretoner Jerry Holland, a fiddler-stepdancer with the ability to impress even the folks back home, and fiddler a frenzy

Buddy MacMaster who led a musical group to the Outer Hebrides.

The Orkney Islands welcomed a pair of Quebec Canadian native Cree fiddlers, whose ancestors had learned Scottish rhythms from the islands' fur traders in Canada. The duo got such a warm reception in Scotland no one thought to ask whether the connection had anything to do with poet Robert Burns' Scotched rendition of old song *The Banks O' Cree.*

You'll also see how Canadian indigenous people have kept alive that blending of Celtic-explorer and Canadian-native tunes, if you tune in to the late Cape Breton Micmac aboriginal Lee Cremo. Lee copped "Best Bow Arm in the World" at Nashville's World Fiddle Championship, and was known for doing 32nd and 64th notes, the kind of quickies you rarely hear about, and good luck catching them when they fly by. He also brought a bagpipe approach to the fiddle, so it's obvious his legacy is going to drone on for some time.

The native theme continues with *Micmac Square Dance Tune*, a piece found in many repertoires, and half-Scottish Canadian musician Don Ross's moniker of Mac-Micmac. Half-Mohawk David Maracle gave us the band Yodeca, with Iroquoian and Celtic flutes winding their way through jazz, bluegrass, Acadian, the tablas and chants of India, and Pow Wow dancers to wow crowds. And in northwest Canada, festival crowds suck up the legacy of how the Athabascan First Nations crowd and those Gaelic fur-traders and explorers fiddled and danced around the Arctic Circle together.

Meanwhile, the country and bluegrass movement in Canada produced several performers who pay tribute to legendary fiddler Don Messer. Alberta band Cowboy Celtic formed around leadman David Wilkie's obsession with Scottish drovers, and their North American range-rider reincarnation. The group also has shown their stuff to the homelands, where "cowboy," it seems, is a slang term for someone who bungles the job. Wilkie and his crew not only disproved that, they also got Outstanding Traditional Western Music Album recognition by The National Cowboy Hall of Fame.

Other Celtic grass-mowers include The Duhks, who also take a funky bow to Breton, Acadian and Afro-Cuban, and the more than adequate Clumsy Lovers from Coquitlam, British Columbia, who give *Sweet Home Alabama* equal time with *Highland Skip* and the bicultural *Paddy's Leather Breeches/Banjo Breakdown.* Provincial neighbors Mad Pudding took classical composer Aaron Copland's *Hoedown* and had fun melding three distinctive C forms of music.

Acadian-French rhythms reel in Quebec with Lennie Gallant, Cajun-bluegrass rockers La Bottine Souriante, and Athanor, who also adopted the Scandinavian *nyckelharpa* to remind us of other Celtic lands. Overall, though, you're more likely to find fiddles, a long and winding string of them all across Canada, with a major stop in Glengarry County, Ontario. Swamped with Scottish Highlanders from 1800 on, the region now is full of bands like The Glengarry Bhoys and Hadrian's Wall, who have left home-and-away stages wondering where their foundations have gone.

As for The Tartan Terrors, they're actually a light-hearted team who sing, pipe and dance away any fears we might have of their name, especially with their *Riverdance* parody, *Lord of the Prance.* Their Scottish-musical kin Enter the Haggis get heavier with the Latin jazz drums and electric guitars they pile on top of Highland aerophones. These kilted "Atholl Highlanders" are not too busy traveling with a *Mexican Scotsman* and playing *Bagpipes on Mars*, to pose the eternal question, "Donald, Where's Yer Trousers?"

Certainly not on The Dole Tinkers, who have the legs and kilts to rival California's Wicked Tinkers as well as Enter the Haggis, and proclaim *We Drink and We Fight* and it's *All For Me Grog*. Pagan Mary, with 12 Pints of Guinness in them, have showed us how to do a *Jig For Toronto*, while many groups sing about the *Drunken Sailor*, and *The Last Saskatchewan Pirate*, too far gone to realize that province is landlocked.

The Dust Rhinos from Winnipeg have said *Cheers To You* with offerings like *Whiskey in the Jar*, *Up Your Kilt*, and *Drowsey Maggie Medley for a Celtic Night*. The band's name defies Celtic connection, which is why they picked up the subtitle "The Irish Rovers on speed." Vancouver's Mutiny Gone Overboard were cheeky enough to be called a Celtic version of Toronto band Barenaked Ladies. "Mutiny" have taken many an *Excursion Around the Bay*, stopping off to visit that that last Saskatchewan pirate, before bidding *Farewell to Nova Scotia*, for *The Hills of Connemara*.

But now we come to the really mutinous movement. Celtic punk proudly continues that tradition of the ancient Keltoi who a) stiffened their manes with lime and grease, b) painted garish rhythms on their bodies, and c) made one hell of a racket. The McGillicuddys of Victoria, B.C. have given us LPS like *Kilt By Death* on Retch Records, while nihilistic neighbours Rant Music, formerly known as McGnarley's Rant, are "Celtic music gone astray" – all the way to songs like *Kamikaze Syllables*, an intriguing indication of the Celts' longrunning literary travels.

When 19th-century poet Robbie Burns figuratively met 1970s British punk band The Sex Pistols, The Real McKenzies were born, loch-shock-and-barrel. Leader Paul McKenzie went for revenge at childhood memories of being made to perform in a kilt, and LPs like *Clash of the Tartans* and *Loch'd and Loaded* are the result.

Real McKenzie member Aaron Chapman shared similar childhood performance memories, but after helping terrorize entire continents for five years with The Macs, cut out to don something called The Town Pants, which may be where Donald finally found his trousers. The Pants' first LP, *Liverdance,* covered everything from maritime rants to showband stuff, while their next, *Piston Baroque*, went into *Hell's Kitchen,* and also showed us how *The Lamenters Lament.*

And now, it's time to just...wind...down a little, and note the lamenting, as well as the celebrating, done by gentler modern mystics. In Canada, harpers and balladeers can be found just about everywhere, with their three strains of *gentraige, goltraige* and *suantraige.* And it's a good thing, too. No Druid in his most demented mode could have dreamed up the extremes of climate this country has, and we need these branches of music to battle the Hag of Winter and summer in the city. And nothing honors ancient Celtic concerns, predictions and predilections like the harp.

The high-profile premiere of the Canadian Celtic harper really began with *The Lady of Shalott* in 1991. Loreena McKennitt's treatment of this Arthurian-Celtic tale of a lady who spins her doom around her, became so identified with the long-haired gowned-of-yore songstress, many had no idea there was a wild-haired 19th-century poet called Alfred Tennyson behind it.

McKennitt, though, looked far beyond Shalott for other places the Celts had left their world mark, and as we know by now, there are a lot of these places. She visited *Santiago de Compostela,* and musically encountered Marco Polo, Venetian-Renaissance *La Serenissima,* the Marrakesh Night Market, did a mummer's dance, and took a *Night Ride Across The Caucasus.* She also created a website bidding entry in 14 languages.

And on that combined mouse-click and harp chord we rest a moment, before launching ourselves into a Celtic explosion that took a regional concern and turned it into a raging river around the world.

*

# Chapter 20

# Riverdancing Into the Future

The years 2004, 2005 and 2006 mark 10th anniversaries of the biggest thing that ever happened to Celtic music.

First came a seven-minute show segment called *Riverdance.* Then, the threat of a tidal wave with the first full-length production of the show. And then its male lead and co-choreographer, Michael Flatley, surfaced and stomped off at the rate of 35 taps per second to create his own Celtic extravaganza, *Lord of the Dance.*

On the eve of Beltane, April 30, 1994, the annual televised Eurovision Song contest in Dublin, Ireland had come to a standstill. The global judges were doing their judging, and a numbed-out audience prepared itself for producer Moya Doherty's musical fill-in segment.

An explosion of sleek hard-shoed dancers with speed-blurred legs, a fiery fairy queen flouncing about, a high-kicking chieftain, all to pounding drums and music that rocked and reeled with abandon – this, folks, was *Riverdance,* and in seven minutes flat the dam of Irish step dance, after decades of rigidity and obscure competitions, had been swept away.

The audience roar was primal enough to recall 3,000 years of Celtic music, and except for a few people who confused things with Handel's *Water Music* and Strauss's *Blue Danube,* they sputtered things like "My God. Ireland is *sexy.*" Millions of TV viewers also got drenched that night, and it didn't need a divining *vate* to foresee what these waters held for the future.

The *Riverdance* music piece swept up Top Ten music charts where it stayed for months, but now Doherty and her deputies knew the world expected a whole lot more, like a two-hour show. It was a draining endeavor, but that gold in the river beckoned, and by February 1995 the first full-length production was flooding Dublin. Its opening number, *Reel Around the Sun,* also became the unofficial theme piece for the show's future, if anyone could have guessed it.

*Riverdance* also introduced a celestial Celtic choir, soft-shoe Irish dance which a stymied media could only identify as "ballet," a bagpipe lament for ancient hero ChuChulainn, some Spanish flamenco with extinguishers in the wings, Russian folk ballet and Eastern European melodrama (the Keltoi did come out of those parts), a rollicking and oh-so-poignant *American Wake* sequence, a huge *Harbour of the New World,* and *Trading Taps*, where Harlem meets hinterland Erin, and some competitive gymnastics result in total understanding.

Female lead Jean Butler was a flame-haired Irish-New Yorker with wings barely folded above mile-high legs, male lead Michael Flatley a tough Irish-Chicagoan, who had begun to free Irish dancing from its spinal-retentive incarceration by moving his arms (the kind of thing that gets you instantly booted from a competition), rolling his pelvis, and doing triple-kicks.

Those who disapproved usually were people who have seen too many old Irish-village crossroads dances, hidebound *feisanna*, and films like *The Quiet Man.* Many felt *Riverdance* was flash over substance, while the opposite side waded up to accuse naysayers of being dead in the water. Some folks simply don't like changing currents, but an impressive number threw themselves right in to this whirlpool of pounding, pattering, swirling rhythms, all the way down to the sea.

When Michael Flatley abruptly left in 1995 amidst dual-camp concerns of "creative control," and Jean Butler hobbled up in crutches, the drowning-preventive was to chant "the show is the star" mantra someone came up with. World-champ Colin Dunne immersed himself, with 20 hours notice, for the extreme challenge. Alternating Butler fill-in goddesses Areleen Boyle and Eileen Martin, one fair, the other dark, also were prize swimmers. Still, the team clutched life preservers while chewing their nails in triple-jig speed, but the standing ovations drowned any fears. The show was the star.

The ups-and-downs got harder when *Riverdance* hit New York's Radio City Music Hall one year later. This is a rarity in the annals of regional productions, and it wasn't exactly a shoe-in here. The stage floor, which had seen many Rockette launches, didn't have the "spring" Riverdancers need.

Massage therapists were reeled in to work overtime, as opening night reeled in famous Irish-Americans like Ted Kennedy and clan, Chevy Chase chasing his Irish roots, and actor Liam Neeson proclaiming to media that it was "Ireland's turn" in the planetary scheme of things. But, asked a reporter, what about the fact this big event was in New York City? Neeson merely replied that, well, the Irish invented New York, which we know by now.

As for the show, it had to duplicate itself to satisfy global demand, and as the news told us, cloning was now possible, and as we also know now, the Celts were big on transcreation. Every element in the show was copied, twice, three times, in separate troupes that went forth on heel-blistering hemispheric schedules. Some lead dancers went spinning off to other shows, some musicians left for new pan-Celtic groups, but there was no shortage of equally flash-footed and fingered performers to hit the stage running. The show was the star.

The Internet offered more *Riverdance* run-off web-sites than there are tributaries on the face of this Earth, and followers also began tapping out demands for a new trivia industry.

We learned for example, that the show's Boyne Company troupe's dancers ranged from 5¼ to 6¼ feet, had 494 years of stepdance training among them, used 3,132 inches of shoelaces, drank 125 gallons of water weekly, got wound up in 32 rolls of self-grip physiotherapists' tape each week, and unwound enough to go through 10,000 individual steps per dancer per show, tapping their way through 15,000 pounds of dry ice each month.

We also learned about dancers' good-luck rituals and occasional slipups during *Reel Around the Sun* and *American Wake,* while another occupational hazard was getting kicked in the hips and thighs (not intentionally), until Ireland had to post new national colours of black and blue.

The speed gauge also went all over, as lead dancer Colin Dunne put out an instructional video, *Celtic Feet,* at a reassuring rate that made you think you could actually do the stuff. Lead Michael Patrick Gallagher speeded up things even more in an ad for Time Warner Cable's Road Runner High Speed Internet Service as "fastest feet" for a TV commercial. Breandan de Gallai simply left a lot in the dust, as he's known as the motor racer of Irish dancing.

There was Riverdancing on the Great Wall of China, a long-running Broadway version, 5000th-Performance Celebrations, a "Flying Squad" to perform at special events, a *Riverdance* Day in cities here and there, and occasional grand come-togethers in, of all places, Ireland. The show also maxed out the color palette in its sleek costumes, but always, for which we can be thankful, spurning the garishness of what the world knew as "Irish dance wear."

With little more than the usual production hitches, *Riverdance* continued flowing along, before coming up against another obstacle. The news that the show augmented its live steps with recorded taps was trumpeted throughout the media. Other Celtic shows did a quick two-step up to claim non-involvement.

But millions of tapped-in fans didn't care. They were the ones filling monster theatres that needed a little enhancement, anyway. And who really is to know other Celtaganzas didn't do some tap-taping of their own? Can they all be that loud on their own?

One thing *Riverdance* was quite open about was its Celtic-rock-band-of-an-orchestra, which was right on-stage, albeit well out of the way of those Donegal-and-beyond dervishes. Those musicians who did come right out next to the dancers for certain segments and beat and blew and fiddled, may have counted life and limb by seconds, but as far as we know there have been no fatalities.

Instruments like the Greek-cum-Irish bouzouki and the strictly Bulgarian *kaval* and *gadulka* (flute and fiddle) came to the forefront. The saxophone was a surprise, but it blew Celtic wind to rival any pipes. Many people thought the music score itself was "existing traditional," for some reason considered the ultimate compliment. But it was all the work of composer Bill Whelan, who had folked around with rock and reel band Planxty, paid musical tribute to Sean O'Riada, and orchestrated Irish chief Red Hugh O'Donnell's 1601 flight to Spain in *Seville Suite*.

Along the way, the video industry got jigging with *Riverdance: The Show* (Dublin), followed by *Riverdance: Live From New York City, Riverdance Live From Geneva* and the documentary treatment *Riverdance: a Journey*, to be updated in *Journey 2,* and possibly *Sons and Daughters of Riverdancers* and *We Won't Let The River Run Dry*.

Meanwhile, Michael Flatley was doing very well with his own extravaganza called, in case we questioned his standing, *Lord of the Dance*. It's also the name of an old hymn, but its new identity was about as subtle as Las Vegas in outer space. Beneath the flash, though, the Good-vs.Evil-themed LOTD paid tribute to Celtic mythology. Ancient characters like Erin the Goddess, dark lord Don Dorcha, the blood-lusty Morrigan and sweet-freedom Saoirse, were revived in downright sexy personifications, all to the tune of composer Ronan Hardiman, who'd scored for Irish lottery commercials and really hit the pot of gold here.

As for the lord of this dance, he had a Golden Glove boxing champ background that punched up a fancy-footwork face-off with the Dark Lord, while Flatley's All-Ireland-Championship flute playing in other segments was the final blow to those who thought he was just a speed freak who'd tapped his way into *The Guinness Book of World Records*.

*Lord of the Dance*, which also underwent the clone-aid experience, began to set its own records, and then got even bigger with its turbo-charged reincarnation *Feet of Flames,* presented one night in the historic Route of Kings, Hyde Park, London. Called the biggest live dance show ever shown, it had over 100 dancers (none cloned) and the kinds of theatrical staging and effects any rock band would gladly trade all its uppers for. The video industry welcomed *Lord of the Dance*, *Feet of Flames*, *Michael Flatley Gold* and *Michael Flatley Collection.*

This global Gael force began to produce other song-and-dance revues, Canada's *Needfire* among them. As the lights came up, Denny Doherty (a Canadian contributor to 1960s folk music in The Mamas and The Papas) was the parental narrator who told us about that ancient Beltane ritual, when everyone lit their fires from one communal flame. In days of yore, Beltane then erupted in song and dance, and this was no different.

The Irish Descendants and other progeny did some male-bonding in a rousing version of *Barrett's Privateers*. Tenor-of-tears John McDermott and Gaelic girls Mary Jane Lamond, the Rankins and The Ennis Sisters poured it on, Newfoundland fiddler Jim Fidler fiddled, John Allan Cameron godfathered it all, and Scottish Highland and step dancers did things high and fast enough to stop Flatley and Co. in their taps.

The Celtic craze also tidal-waved players like Canadian country-rock diva Shania Twain, who waded right in to her video, *Don't Be Stupid,* with some fancy footwork, while the Pointy-Haired Boss of comic-strip character *Dilbert* missed an important deadline because he'd been sucked up into a vortex of "Irish line dancing lessons." The same thing was happening to people all over the world, including adults who until then had grumbled about getting up to change channels.

And as *Riverdance* and *Lord of the Dance* gear up in 2005 and 2006 to celebrate 10 years of full-flung stagedom, there are many other song-and-dance revues no doubt aiming for the decade mark.

Like its predecessors, *Ragus* went into the musical lab to split off into equal troupes, *Rhythm of the Dance* debuted in the debatably-Celtic land of Norway, *Magic of the Dance* beefed up the emigrant experience, *Dance of Desire* dished up Arabian, Hungarian and tango amongst the Irish. *Lord of the Flames* was mostly Spanish, *Gaelforce Dance* was a force to reckon with, and things ultimately went from African-Appalachian production *SoulMates* all the way up *To Dance On The Moon*.

It all got bigger and faster and bolder and bustier, with doubled and tripled and quadrupled troupes reeling around the universe and trying to outshoe, outshow and outshine each other. Fortunately, these shows do have quieter moments where some poignant musical pondering on love, loss, history, herstory and mythology gets center stage.

## CLOSING

We might as well do some pondering ourselves as we come to the end, which is really a "To be continued..." because who knows what forms Celtic music will take tomorrow?

This 3000-year-old tradition has been sanctified, countryfied, Classic-fied, multicultured, sleep-strained, synthesized, rocked up, and punked out, and generally revived, reinvented, rehabilitated and reborn.

The Internet has assaulted Celtophiles around the known world with it, with, even, online-interactive music tutorial programs manned by masters of fiddle, bodhran, bagpipes and other instruments. As the Celts always were known for being innovators and inventors, there's no telling where this will end.

Of one thing we can be sure, though, and it's something the Net can't replicate yet. On almost any night somewhere around the world, there's a darkened stage, with the dark sound of low-whistle haunting its way through enough smoke and mist to alert emergency services.

Light infuses the stage as lithe figures roll their heads to the sun, then explodes as these Lugh-worshippers come to life with flashing legs and flying hair. The wailing winds, strings and drums of an onstage orchestra begin their *oran mhor* assault as dancers begin to wheel and reel around the sun, and the rhythms go all over the place as the show morphs into a multiCeltural panorama and more.

*Riverdance* says it all. This is World Music. Sure as *sidhe,* it's three millennia old. But the pipes are droning, the *ceili's* calling, the needfire's burning, and sorry folks, but musically speaking it's really just the *craic* of dawn here.

✼✼✼

# Index

177

183

# About the Author

Winnie Czulinski is a phonetically-obsessed writer, researcher and publicist who would have you know that "Cz" is pronounced "Ch." This Celtophile has written for many North American and British magazines, books, companies and offbeat concerns.

Because she was overwhelmed by the stage production *Riverdance* in 1997, though, she never quite found her way back up from underwater. Her love of other Celtic extravaganzas such as *Lord of the Dance* & *Needfire* also have inspired this book.

As musician "Winnie, Lady of the Dulcimer," she plays the world's most multiCeltural instrument, the mountain dulcimer. She has created video and documentary soundtrack music, and performs at many arts, corporate and historical events. Her musical inspiration includes Bill Whelan and Ronan Hardiman (composers of *Riverdance* and *Lord of the Dance*), Canadian world musician Loreena McKennitt, and classical-&-film composer Miklos Rozsa.

When Winnie is not immersed in her computer, dulcimer, Celtic videos and her family, she can be found maxing-out libraries and taking very long walks to figure out knotty passages in her latest composition.

Winnie Czulinski looks forward to your questions, comments, subjects and predilections, and can be reached at: celticwinnie@yahoo.ca

Front cover illustration *Der Dudelsackpfeifer*
(The Bagpiper) by German artist Albrecht Dürer, 1514.

Drone On! The High History of Celtic Music
Copyright © Winnie Czulinski, 2004

First published in Canada by
Sound And Vision
359 Riverdale Avenue
Toronto, Canada, M4J 1A4
www.soundandvision.com
First printing, July 2004
1 3 5 7 9 - printings - 10 8 6 4 2


National Library and Archives Canada
Cataloguing in Publication

Czulinski, Winnie, 1956-
Drone on! : The high history of Celtic music /
Winnie Czulinski ;

ISBN 0-920151-39-6

1. Celtic music—History and criticism.  2. Celtic music—
Humor.  I. Title.
ML3650.C997 2004      781.62'916      C2004-903263-1


Typset in Bookman Old Style
Printed and bound in Canada

Quotable Books

*Quotable War Or Peace*
Compiled & Edited by Geoff Savage
Caricatures by Mike Rooth
isbn 0-920151-57-4

*Quotable Pop*
Fifty Decades of Blah Blah Blah
Compiled & Edited by Phil Dellio & Scott Woods
Caricatures by Mike Rooth
isbn 0-920151-50-7

*Quotable Jazz*
Compiled & Edited by Marshall Bowden
Caricatures by Mike Rooth
isbn 0-920151-55-8

*Quotable Opera*
Compiled & Edited by Steve & Nancy Tanner
Caricatures by Umberto Tàccola
isbn 0-920151-54-X

*Quotable Alice*
Compiled & Edited by David W. Barber
Illustrations by Sir John Tenniel
isbn 0-920151-52-3

*Quotable Sherlock*
Compiled & Edited by David W. Barber
Illustrations by Sidney Paget
isbn 0-920151-53-1

*Quotable Twain*
Compiled & Edited by David W. Barber
isbn 0-920151-56-6

Other Books

*The Composers*
A Hystery of Music
by Kevin Reeves
preface by Daniel Taylor
isbn 0-920151-29-9

*1812 And All That*
A Concise History of Music from
30.000 B.C to the Millennium
by Lawrence Leonard,
cartoons by Emma Bebbington
isbn 0-920151-33-7

*How to Stay Awake*
During Anybody's Second Movement
by David E. Walden, cartoons by Mike Duncan
preface by Charlie Farquharson
isbn 0-920151-20-5

*How To Listen To Modern Music*
Without Earplugs
by David E. Walden, cartoons by Mike Duncan
foreword by Bramwell Tovey
isbn 0-920151-31-0

*The Thing I've Played With the Most*
Professor Anthon E. Darling Discusses
His Favourite Instrument
by David E. Walden, cartoons by Mike Duncan
foreword by Mabel May Squinnge, B.O.
isbn 0-920151-35-3

Other Books, Cont

*More Love Lives of the Great Composers*
by Basil Howitt
isbn 0-920151-36-1

*Love Lives of the Great Composers*
From Gesualdo to Wagner
by Basil Howitt
isbn 0-920151-18-3

*Opera Antics & Annecdotes*
by Stephen Tanner
Illustrations by Umberto Tàccola
preface by David W. Barber
isbn 0-920151-32-9

*I Wanna Be Sedated*
Pop Music in the Seventies
by Phil Dellio & Scott Woods
Caricatures by Dave Prothero
preface by Chuck Eddy
isbn 0-920151-16-7

*A Working Musician's Joke Book*
by Daniel G. Theaker
Cartoons by Mike Freen
preface by David Barber
isbn 0-920151-23-X

*Grabbing Operas by Their Tales*
*Liberating the Libretti*
by Charles E. Lake
Illustrations by Mike Rooth
isbn 0-920151-38-8

## Note from the Publisher

Sound And Vision books may be purchased for educational or promotional use or for special sales. If you have any comments on this book or any other books we publish, or if you would like a catalogue, please write or email us at.
Sound And Vision
359 Riverdale Avenue,
Toronto, Canada M4J 1A4.
We are always looking for original books to publish. If you have an idea or manuscript that is in the genre of musical humour including educational themes, please contact us. Thank you for purchasing or borrowing this book.
To view our catalogue online, please visit us at:
www.soundandvision.com.

Geoff Savage
Publisher

The Publisher welcomes any information regarding errors or omissions, that we may make necessary corrections in subsequent printings.

MEMBER OF SCABRINI MEDIA

Quebec, Canada
2004